# Group's Fiesta!
## Where kids are fired up about Jesus

# Sing & Play Olé

## Leader Manual

# Group

Loveland, Colorado
www.groupvbs.com

# Group resources actually work!

This Group resource helps you focus on **"The 1 Thing™"**— a life-changing relationship with Jesus Christ. "The 1 Thing" incorporates our **R.E.A.L.** approach to ministry. It reinforces a growing friendship with Jesus, encourages long-term learning, and results in life transformation, because it's:

**Relational**
Learner-to-learner interaction enhances learning and builds Christian friendships.

**Experiential**
What learners experience through discussion and action sticks with them up to 9 times longer than what they simply hear or read.

**Applicable**
The aim of Christian education is to equip learners to be both hearers and doers of God's Word.

**Learner-based**
Learners understand and retain more when the learning process takes into consideration how they learn best.

Note: The price of this Sing & Play Olé Leader Manual includes the right for you to make as many copies of the five "Frieda's Fiesta Adventure" skits as you need for your vacation Bible school. If another church or organization wants copies of these skits, it must purchase Group's Fiesta in order to receive performance rights.

**Sing & Play Olé Leader Manual**
Copyright © 2006 Group Publishing, Inc.

Visit our Web sites:
**www.group.com**
**www.groupvbs.com**
**www.groupoutlet.com**

**Thanks to our talented VBS curriculum team!**
Jessica Broderick, Jody Brolsma, Shelly Dillon, Heather A. Eades, Cindy S. Hansen, Elisa Hansen, Lisa Harris, Tracy K. Hindman, Alison Imbriaco, Mikal Keefer, Scott Kinner, Maura Link, Linda Marcinkowski, Kari K. Monson, Barbie Murphy, Amy Nappa, Peggy Naylor, Jane Parenteau, Janis Sampson, Joani Schultz, Pamela Shoup, Rodney Stewart, Kelli B. Trujillo

Unless otherwise noted, all Scripture quotations are taken from the *Holy Bible*, New Living Translation, copyright © 1996, 2004. Used by permission of Tyndale House Publishers, Inc., Wheaton, Illinois 60189. All rights reserved.

ISBN 978-0-7644-2951-4
Printed in the United States of America.
10 9 8 7 6 5 4 3 2 1      08 07 06

# Group's Fiesta!
### Where kids are fired up about Jesus

# Sing & Play Olé

## CONTENTS

# Hola, Amigos! Welcome to Fiesta!

Welcome to Fiesta, where kids are fired up about Jesus! Get ready for an exciting celebration of Jesus' love filled with lively mariachi bands, colorful *folklorico* costumes, spicy chili peppers, and warm friends.

Fiesta is overflowing with fun for kids, teenagers, and adults. Everyone involved in *this* VBS will jump into God's Word…and will never be the same again! As kids explore amazing Bible adventures, they'll take part in Daily Challenges that encourage them to apply Bible truths to everyday life.

If you haven't used Group's VBS materials before, you're in for a real celebration. Fiesta is an exciting, fun-filled, Bible-based program your kids will love. (We know because we tested everything in a field test last summer. Look for the "Fiesta Findings" to learn how our discoveries will make *your* program the best!)

Kids start each day by forming small groups called Fiesta Crews. All the Fiesta Crews gather at Sing & Play Olé to sing and do fun motions to upbeat Bible songs that introduce kids to the concepts they'll be learning that day. Then Fiesta Crews visit five different Fiesta Stations.

They sample tasty treats at Maraca Munchies, go on Hot Bible Adventures, make delightful creations in Cactus Crafts, play Grande Games, and meet Chadder Chipmunk™ on video! Then everyone comes together for the closing, Fiesta Finale.

During Sing & Play Olé, kids worship with fun actions as they sing easy-to-learn Bible songs. Kids will love the theme song, "Never Be the Same!" and the other VBS songs. The *Sing & Play Olé Music* audiocassette or CD, lyrics transparencies (from the *Fiesta! Clip Art, Song Lyrics, and Decorating* CD), and a *Sing & Play Olé Music* video all make your job a snap! (The CDs, audiocassette, video, and a DVD are available from Group Publishing or your local Group supplier.)

Thanks for leading Sing & Play Olé! Your Fiesta Station is the first one kids visit each day. When kids come to Sing & Play Olé, they'll worship with unforgettable songs that reinforce the daily Bible Point. After worshipping at Sing & Play Olé, everyone can start the day with a smile.

## Leading Sing & Play Olé is easy and fun!

You'll enjoy your role and be most successful as a Sing & Play Olé Leader if you

- have experience leading songs or singing with children,
- enjoy seeing kids "get into" the music—but not for the sake of performance and perfection,
- can motivate and energize kids,
- are comfortable in front of large groups,
- are active and energetic, and
- model Jesus' love in everything you say and do.

### FIESTA FINDINGS

*One of the greatest things about this VBS program is that kids actually get to worship! Everyone in our field test loved the idea that kids of all ages could come together and enjoy singing just to praise God rather than to rehearse for a performance.*

### FIESTA FINDINGS

*We've discovered that it does help to have a high-energy, cheerful leader for Sing & Play Olé. The leader at our field test kept kids active and engaged in each song and heaped affirmation on kids between songs! Have fun, and keep things moving as you introduce kids to Fiesta.*

# Fiesta Overview

| | Bible Point | Bible Story | Treasure Verse | Sing & Play Olé | Hot Bible Adventures | Grande Games |
|---|---|---|---|---|---|---|
| **DAY 1** | Jesus is our friend. | Men bring their friend to Jesus for healing (Luke 5:17-25). | "Now you are my friends" (John 15:15). | • Introduce the Bible story of the men bringing their friend to Jesus for healing. • Introduce Ray the sun Bible Memory Buddy. • Help kids choose Fiesta Crew jobs. • Teach: "Never Be the Same!" "No, Not One/What a Friend We Have in Jesus" "I Have a Friend" "We Want to See Jesus Lifted High" | Men bring their friend to Jesus for healing. • Try to eat pretzels with "paralyzed" arms. • Discover how some men brought their friend to Jesus. | **Play:** • Friendship Mat Relay • Ice Melt • Amigo Art |
| **DAY 2** | Jesus is our life. | Jesus raises Lazarus from the dead (John 11:1-44). | "And you must love the Lord your God with all your heart" (Deuteronomy 6:5). | • Introduce the Bible story about Jesus raising Lazarus from the dead. • Introduce Rosa the jack rabbit Bible Memory Buddy. • Teach: "I'm Gonna Clap My Hands" "I Got the Joy" "Trading My Sorrows" | Jesus raises Lazarus from the dead. • Meet Lazarus' friend…and then meet a living Lazarus! • Discover that Jesus was Lazarus' life, and he's our life, too. | **Play:** • Hands Filled With Distractions • Lazarus, Come Out! • Shrinking Blankets |
| **DAY 3** | Jesus is our leader. | Jesus chooses his first disciples (Matthew 4:18-22). | "Jesus called out to them, 'Come, follow me!'" (Matthew 4:19). | • Introduce the Bible story about Jesus calling the disciples. • Introduce Cody the coyote Bible Memory Buddy. • Teach: "King Jesus Is All" "Help Me, Jesus" | Jesus chooses his first disciples. • Meet Zebedee and apply for fishermen jobs. • Convince Zebedee why his sons would follow Jesus and why we follow Jesus, too. | **Play:** • Caliente! • Hot Tamales • Got-Cha-Cha Tag |
| **DAY 4** | Jesus is our Savior. | Jesus dies and rises again (John 19:17–20:29). | "Since I live, you also will live" (John 14:19). | • Introduce the Bible story about Jesus dying and rising again. • Introduce Spike the cactus Bible Memory Buddy. • Teach: "You Gave" | Jesus dies and rises again. • Crawl through a cave, and hide from Romans. • Learn that Jesus died and rose again—Jesus is our Savior. | **Play:** • Cactus Patch • Spike Tag • Confetti Drop |
| **DAY 5** | Jesus is our helper. | Ananias helps Saul (Acts 9:1-19). | "The Lord is my helper, so I will have no fear" (Hebrews 13:6). | • Introduce the Bible story about Ananias helping Saul. • Introduce Pablo the chili pepper Bible Memory Buddy. • Review Sing & Play Olé songs. | Ananias helps Saul. • Help the leader not be afraid to help Saul. • See Saul's eyes healed. | **Play:** • Blind Help • Canteen Fill-Up • Chili Pepper Chasers |

| Maraca Munchies | Chadder's Desert Drive-in Theater | Cactus Crafts and Missions | Fiesta Finale |
|---|---|---|---|
| Fiesta Friendship Cake | Chadder begins his journey through the hot desert with his friend Miranda. They're on their way to her Grandpa Luis' fiesta birthday party. Will Chadder and Miranda make it through the desert? | • Amigo Pack | • Review the Treasure Verse (John 15:15) from the Bible.<br>• Bring "Buddy," a balloon friend, to Jesus.<br>• Sing songs to celebrate our friend Jesus.<br>• Take home Daily Challenge reminders to show others that Jesus is our friend. |
| Rosa Rabbits | Chadder and Miranda befriend Alfonso. They don't realize that the wacky sheriff and his campaign manager want to get the sheriff re-elected. To do this, the sheriff and Ms. Stickler decide to protect their town from a dangerous criminal—Chadder! | • Sun Shakers<br><br>• Fiesta Sun Catchers | • Review the Treasure Verse (Deuteronomy 6:5).<br>• Play with a piñata, and wait for a surprise.<br>• Pray, sing, and celebrate that Jesus is our life.<br>• Take home Daily Challenge reminders to show others that Jesus is our life. |
| "Where Did They Go?" Boats | During a confusing speech by the bumbling sheriff, Chadder gets a taste of some super-hot sauce. Smoke comes out of his ears! Before we know it, Chadder, Miranda, and Alfonso are in jail! | • Follow-the-Leader Swivel Streamers<br><br>• Howlin' Coyote Key Chain | • Review the Treasure Verse (Matthew 4:19).<br>• Participate in an instant re-enactment of today's Bible story.<br>• Sing songs, thanking Jesus for being our leader.<br>• Take home Daily Challenge reminders to show others that Jesus is our leader. |
| Fiesta Fun Fruit Kabob | The friends try to tell the sheriff they're innocent, but he doesn't believe them. Alfonso escapes—without water and without knowing the direction to Grandpa Luis' fiesta. Will Chadder and Miranda get to Alfonso in time? | • Mariachi Maracas<br><br>• Etch-a-Frame Photo Frames | • Thank Jesus for his beautiful gift of eternal life.<br>• Review the Treasure Verse (John 14:19).<br>• Sing worshipful songs as they thank Jesus for being our Savior.<br>• Take home Daily Challenge reminders to show others that Jesus is our Savior. |
| Saul's Seeing Eyes | All's well that ends well. Alfonso is saved in the desert, the friends make it to Grandpa Luis' fiesta birthday party, and the real criminal is caught. Watch the video to find out who the real criminal is! (It's not Chadder!) | • Boppaloons<br><br>• Pepper Pals | • Remember what they've learned at Fiesta.<br>• Review the Treasure Verse (Hebrews 13:6).<br>• Present their Operation Kid-to-Kid books and blankets as an offering to God.<br>• Take home Daily Challenge reminders to show others that Jesus is our helper. |

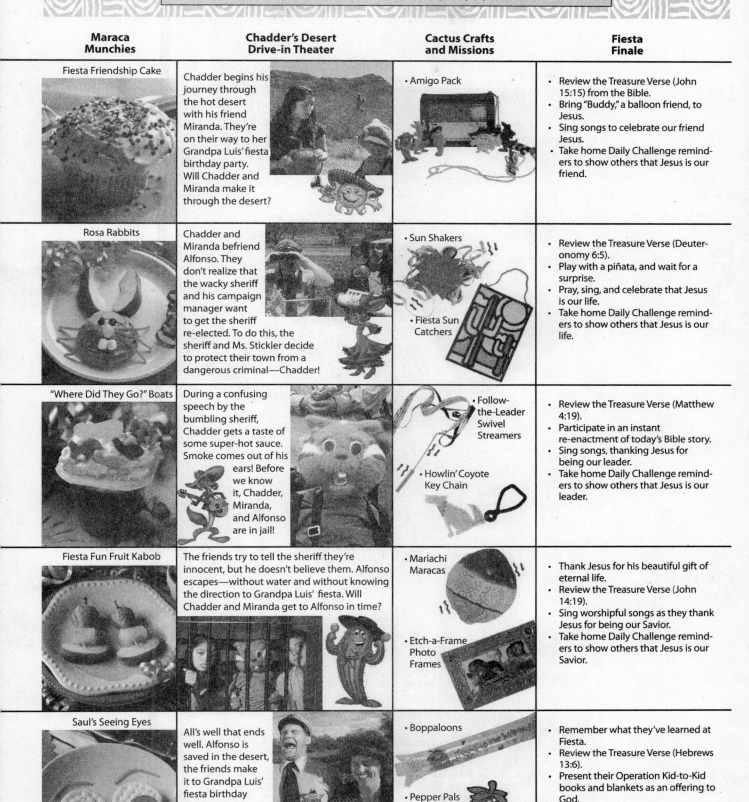

# Fiesta Is Jumping With New Friends!

Each day at Fiesta, kids meet an adorable buddy who reminds them of the day's Bible Point. They're Bible Memory Buddies®! We'll let our fun friends speak for themselves.

**Spike here.** My needles remind us of the nails they put in Jesus' hands when he died for us. I'm glad Jesus is our Savior.

**It's me . . . Rosa!** We jack rabbits like to hop around. I'm jumping for joy because Jesus is our life.

**Hi, amigos! I'm Ray,** the warm, friendly sun. I'll remind kids that Jesus is our friend!

**My name's Pablo!** Chili peppers help make food spicy. I'm fired up that Jesus is our helper.

**Hey, it's Cody the Coyote!** Some coyotes follow the leader of their pack. I want kids to follow Jesus, who is our leader.

To help kids remember these important Bible truths, the Chadder's Desert Drive-In Theater Leader will give each child a Bible Memory Buddy every day to keep in his or her Amigo Pack (an awesome craft that kids make on Day 1). And each Buddy has the Treasure Verse inscribed on it. Kids will *love* collecting these buddies! And you'll be amazed at how the Bible Memory Buddies help kids apply Bible truths to everyday life.

# Your Role at Fiesta

Here's what's expected of you before, during, and after Group's Fiesta.

## Before Fiesta

- **Attend scheduled station leader training.**

- **Pray for the kids who will attend your church's Fiesta.**

- **Plan your wardrobe.** Ask your Fiesta Director (otherwise known as your church's VBS director) what you should wear. Adult staff T-shirts (available from Group Publishing or your local Group supplier) will help kids identify you and help you identify other station leaders. Or wear bright-colored hats and shirts for a fiesta look!

- **Read this Sing & Play Olé Leader Manual.**

- **Decide if you'll use the "Frieda's Fiesta Adventure" scripts in your program.** The voices and sound effects are recorded on the *Fiesta! Skits & Drama* CD. All you'll need are two volunteers to act out the leading characters' roles each day. The leading characters could even be puppets—just have volunteers work the puppets while you play the words and sound effects on the CD. It's so easy; your volunteers don't even have to speak!

- **Check all equipment to make sure it's working properly.**

- **Watch the *Sing & Play Olé Music* video.** Besides being fun to watch, it's a great way to see the motions. (You can use the video to teach the kids, too! Then you can have kids lead kids.)

- **Learn the songs by using the *Sing & Play Olé Music* audiocassette or CD, the *Sing & Play Olé Music* video, or pages 51-63 in this manual,** where the motions are described next to the lyrics. You'll want to be familiar with all of the songs and motions so that you can teach them with ease. (We've heard from VBS song leaders who start using the songs in Sunday school months before VBS starts!)

- **After you've learned the motions to the songs, decide how you'll set up your daily Sing & Play Olé program to best accommodate your staff and the facilities.** The following suggestions will get you started:

  - **Use the *Sing & Play Olé Music* audiocassette or CD.** All of the songs that you'll use at Sing & Play Olé are included on the audiocassette and CD. Kids will enjoy singing along with the children's voices on the audiocassette or CD, and the vocals will make it easier to learn each song. The CD includes instrumental versions of the songs, so you can use only the accompaniment if you prefer. Once children know the words, the beat will really help them get into the music.

  - **Use the Sing & Play Olé piano or guitar accompaniment in this manual.** The sheet music to all of the Sing & Play Olé songs is printed beginning on page 67. You can also use the sheet music to incorporate VBS songs into other children's ministry programming.

  - **Make your own Sing & Play Olé lyrics transparencies, or make a PowerPoint presentation.** You can print out the song lyrics from the *Fiesta! Clip Art, Song Lyrics, and Decorating* CD and copy them onto transparencies. (Remember that, although the transparencies make it easy for *leaders* to learn the words, many of

*Station leader training is very important! Even VBS veterans will gain new insights and tips for being spectacular station leaders. Don't miss this great opportunity to learn how to make your lessons really stick!*

*We've intentionally kept the dramas simple so they're easy for churches of all sizes to put on. However, some VBS directors love to do more elaborate dramas. Go for it! Give Frieda another left-behind shopping buddy who's just as wacky as she is, or have additional cast dress up as fun characters that Frieda meets. Just remember to keep the humor simple and follow a basic story line that kids can keep up with. Use your creativity to elaborate on these simple skits.*

*You'll find that a CD is the way to go! It's simple to use because finding the beginning of each song is so easy. Many CD players can be programmed to play the day's songs in order.*

*You may be tempted to integrate music from your regular children's ministry. While we're sure you've got some great favorites, the Fiesta songs have been specially chosen to emphasize each day's Bible Point. Plus, kids will enjoy a week of special music!*

**FIESTA FINDINGS**

*Crew leaders at our field tests always ask for the lyrics transparencies at the beginning of the week. But by the middle of the week, they're amazed at how quickly kids learn the songs—without having lyrics in front of them! Turn up the CD player, and let the CD teach the songs! Don't worry about getting every word right. Help kids learn the motions first (they're so easy!), and the words will come. It works!*

**RED HOT TIPS**

*You may notice that the Sing & Play Olé material doesn't include song sheets for the children. That's because the Sing & Play Olé songs and motions are so easy and fun that your kids will learn them right away. Simply say the words as you demonstrate the motions and then invite kids to join in! We believe it's most important for kids to experience the music. The words will come!*

the kids at your VBS won't be able to read well enough to follow along.) If you choose, you can make a PowerPoint presentation instead of transparencies.

- **Choose a child each day to display the Bible Point poster.** You'll need a picture of each of the five Bible Memory Buddies® (buddies that help kids remember the Bible Points and Treasure Verses). Bible Point posters with these Fiesta friends are available from Group Publishing or your local Group supplier. You can also find pictures of the Bible Memory Buddies on the *Fiesta! Clip Art, Song Lyrics, and Decorating* CD. Simply print out the pictures as large (and as bright) as possible, and attach the pictures to large sheets of poster board or foam core. Throughout the week, review the Bible Points from the previous days.

  You'll find suggestions for having kids assist by holding the posters, holding another Bible Point reminder, or pantomiming the Bible Point. These assistants can also help you lead the theme song.

- **You may want to recruit a Sing & Play Olé band of five or six energetic children, teenagers, or adults to help you lead the singing each day.** Be sure the band meets ahead of time to learn and become comfortable with the songs and motions. Having lots of helpers up front adds visual excitement to Sing & Play Olé.

- **For Day 1, consider having the other station leaders help you lead the theme song.** Before VBS, ask the station leaders to learn the motions.

- **Check with your Fiesta Director to see how many songs you should plan for Day 1.** Since some kids will complete registration earlier than others, you'll probably want to begin singing *before* the scheduled start time. This manual suggests warm-up songs so that kids who arrive early can start singing about 10 minutes before your Fiesta begins each day. (And be sure to have music playing as kids arrive. The music really helps to set an upbeat, fun, and energetic tone for your day!) If you start earlier, you may want to add other songs that the kids in your church are familiar with. You can even take requests!

- **Meet with the Fiesta Finale Leader.** Each day's Fiesta Finale will be a fun, involving review of the day's Bible story. The Fiesta Finale Leader will need all the station leaders available to make things go smoothly. He or she will call on you to lead the singing each day, but you should also be prepared to assist with distributing, displaying, or collecting props as needed.

- **To reinforce the daily Bible Points and add to the fun at your VBS, arrange to play Sing & Play Olé music at each station and in the hallways between activities.** Check your Fiesta catalog for new, lower prices on audiocassettes and CDs.

I know you'll want this sizzling, red hot, important information!

**IMPORTANT LEGAL INFORMATION**

When you buy a *Sing & Play Olé Music* audiocassette or CD or a *Sing & Play Olé Music* video, you also buy the right to use the 10 Fiesta songs. You're welcome to play these songs as often as you like. But companies that own these songs haven't given you (or us) permission to duplicate any of your Sing & Play Olé products. Making your own copies—even to use at Fiesta—is against the law, which is a fact many people don't know.

If you'd like to make transparencies or a PowerPoint presentation of the song lyrics, you can purchase the *Fiesta! Clip Art, Song Lyrics, and Decorating* CD. The song lyrics on the CD may be used once, by permission of the copyright owner, to make either transparencies or a PowerPoint presentation. Making both electronic and transparency versions is a violation of contract and is strictly prohibited.

- **Welcome everyone to Sing & Play Olé.** You'll be the first station leader kids see each day, so remember to be cheerful and upbeat. Smile! Make a welcoming first impression that sets the tone for the day.

- **To help create a fun atmosphere and reinforce Bible learning, play the *Sing & Play Olé Music* audiocassette or CD as kids enter and leave the room.** If you're using the audiocassette, be sure to rewind it afterward to be ready for the next song you'll sing.

- **Repeat the Bible Point often.** It's important to say the Bible Point just as it's written. Repeating the Bible Point again and again will help children remember it and apply it to their lives. Kids will be listening for the Bible Point so they can respond by shouting "Viva!" Have kids throw their hands up in the air to make a V as they shout "Viva!" Each day's session suggests ways to include the Bible Point.

"Viva!"

- **Lead kids in one or two warm-up songs each day.** Starting the warm-up songs about 10 minutes before your program is scheduled to begin will get early arrivals active right away and will encourage everyone to be on time—maybe even early!

- **Introduce each day's Bible Point and Bible story.** You won't be the only leader who will state the Bible Point, but you'll be the *first!* It's important that kids hear the Bible Point at Sing & Play Olé each day so that they'll arrive at the stations ready to learn (and ready to respond with a resounding *Viva!*).

- **As you introduce the Bible Point and Bible story, hold up a Bible.** Tell kids that the Bible story comes from God's Word, and mention the specific book in the Bible the story comes from.

- **Before you sing each song, teach kids the new motions or briefly review the motions they've already learned.** Encourage the kids to do the motions, but don't force or embarrass anyone. (Some kids aren't comfortable doing motions as they sing. But you may find that even shy kids forget to be self-conscious because they're having so much fun!)

- **Know the songs well, and know motions well enough to call out each motion just before kids should begin doing it.** (This really does help!)

- **Let the recorded voices on the *Sing & Play Olé Music* audiocassette or CD carry the words at first.** *It's not important that the children know the words for the first couple of days.* Instead, let children enjoy the beat and sounds as they sing along. The words will come naturally soon enough! (Here's a tip: Think of singing with the CD or audiocassette as using a karaoke machine.)

- **Although there's no set time for the "Frieda's Fiesta Adventure" skit, plan to sing one or two songs before you do the daily skit.** That way, latecomers won't miss any of the action in the skit.

### FIESTA FINDINGS

*It may be a past VBS tradition to do music as one rotation or class so that you do it with a smaller group of kids. We strongly recommend that you do this Sing & Play Olé session as it's written—with everyone together. The opening worship time is a highlight of our field test each year. With all the kids together, the energy is electric. This time is designed to be a high-energy, exciting time of worship for kids. It's hard to duplicate that kind of enthusiasm when only some of your kids are taking part. (And don't worry about kids learning the music—it'll be integrated into many other stations each day!)*

### RED HOT TIPS

*You may be tempted to fall back on the old "let's see who can sing the loudest" competition. We'd encourage you to steer clear of competitions like this...particularly during Sing & Play Olé. Remember to keep the focus on upbeat praise and worship rather than a screaming match between kids. You have the opportunity to demonstrate how exciting and energetic our praises can be.*

### FIESTA FINDINGS

*Don't make perfect motions the focus of your Sing & Play Olé time. Briefly explain the motions and what they mean, and then move on. Remember, the kids are here to worship—the motions are just another way for kids to praise God!*

- **Be flexible.** You'll probably need to adapt the Sing & Play Olé sessions to accommodate longer or shorter periods of time—especially if registration runs late on the first day. Each day's Sing & Play Olé program has been designed to last 20 to 25 minutes.

- **At the end of each day's Sing & Play Olé, invite your VBS director to come to the front.** He or she can share announcements, pray, and then dismiss kids in an orderly manner: first the elementary kids, a few Fiesta Crews at a time, and then the preschoolers (who will need a little more time than the big kids to exit).

- **Lead the singing during Fiesta Finale.** Check with the Fiesta Finale Leader to find out which songs you'll lead each day.

## After Fiesta

- Return equipment to its proper place. Return the *Sing & Play Olé Music* audiocassette or CD, the *Sing & Play Olé Music* video, and the lyrics transparencies to your director.

- Throughout the year, keep kids fired up about Jesus' love by

  - phoning neighborhood kids who participated in your Fiesta program,

  - sending follow-up postcards,

  - having Frieda make a surprise appearance at another children's ministry event, and

  - singing "Never Be the Same!" and other Sing & Play Olé songs at other children's ministry events.

# What to Expect at Fiesta

If this is your first time using Group's VBS, you're in for a real treat. You're also in for some surprises! If you look beneath the surface, you'll discover that this VBS program is unlike any you've ever seen or experienced.

| You might expect to see... | But at Fiesta, you'll see... | That's because... |
|---|---|---|
| kids quietly working in workbooks. | kids talking excitedly in their Fiesta Crews. | crew leaders and station leaders will encourage kids to talk about important Bible truths to cement them to their lives. |
| a traditional school setting, with desks or tables. | kids sitting in small, knee-to-knee circles (maybe even on the floor!). | we want kids to get face to face as they talk about how to apply God's Word to their lives. (And it's just plain easier for kids to sit on the floor instead of in chairs!) |
| children in age-graded classrooms. | children in mixed-age groups called Fiesta Crews. | kids will learn so much more by interacting with children of different ages. Think of each crew as a mini-family. |
| classes that look neat and orderly. | lots of child-friendly movement, activity, and energy—and a little clutter, too! | we know that kids have a lot of energy—so each activity is designed to let kids actively participate in fun and exciting ways (the way kids are designed to learn!). |
| kids spending most of their time in one classroom. | Fiesta Crews traveling from station to station about every 20 minutes. | station leaders prepare only about 20 minutes of activities. Not only is that easier on leaders like you, but it keeps kids busy—so there's no time to get into trouble! |
| kids memorizing Bible verses to receive prizes. | kids learning—and understanding—God's Word like you've never seen before! | Bible learning should be *meaningful, delightful,* and *unforgettable.* |

# What's the Daily Challenge®?

## RED HOT TIPS

You'll find the Fiesta stickers on your sticker sheet.

## FIESTA FINDINGS

*Remember that your goal is to encourage kids to practice what they're learning just for the joy of serving Jesus! Don't offer bribes, incentives, or crew competitions to entice kids to complete their Daily Challenges. We discovered that kids didn't need any other motivation—they were excited about choosing a Daily Challenge and living it out! Focus on intrinsic motivation (from the heart), not extrinsic motivation (for external factors).*

## Daily Challenge®

Of course you want kids to come to Fiesta and get fired up about Jesus. But imagine how life changing their experience would be if kids took what they learned, applied it *right away* to daily life, and showed Jesus' love in real life.

That's where the Daily Challenge® comes in! It's as easy as 1, 2, 3!

1. **Build the Daily Challenge® Poles.** Work with your Fiesta Director to build Daily Challenge Poles for your Sing & Play Olé area. For the ultimate in ease, use PVC pipes and fishing line (see the next page in this manual or pages 20-21 in the Director Manual for building tips).

2. **Let kids choose their Daily Challenge.** While kids eat their Maraca Munchies, they will look over that day's Daily Challenges, found in the back of each Fiesta Bible Book. Crew members will work together to choose which challenge they'll do before they come back to Fiesta Finale.

At the end of the day, the Fiesta Finale Leader will have elementary kids take that day's Daily Challenge from their Fiesta Bible Books. Kids will look at the Daily Challenge again to help them remember what challenge they chose. Then each child will fold the Daily Challenge in half lengthwise and use a Fiesta sticker to hold it around the wrist. Each day, kids will wear a new Daily Challenge home!

3. **Watch the Daily Challenge® Flags fly high!** Before Day 2, you or the VBS director will place a Daily Challenge Flag and some tape in each Crew Bag. Starting on Day 2, you (as the Sing & Play Olé Leader) will ask kids to gather with their crews and talk about how they carried out their Daily Challenge. Crews will take out their flag as they share. At a designated time, crew leaders will lower the line from the Daily Challenge Poles and tape their flags to the line. As the lines of Daily Challenge Flags are raised, VBS participants will sing "We Want to See Jesus Lifted High."

**What a great way to "lift Jesus high" throughout your community!**

# Building Your Daily Challenge® Poles

In order to show kids that they're spreading Jesus' love around through the Daily Challenges, you'll need to prepare Daily Challenge Poles in the Sing & Play Olé area. Here's how we made ours.

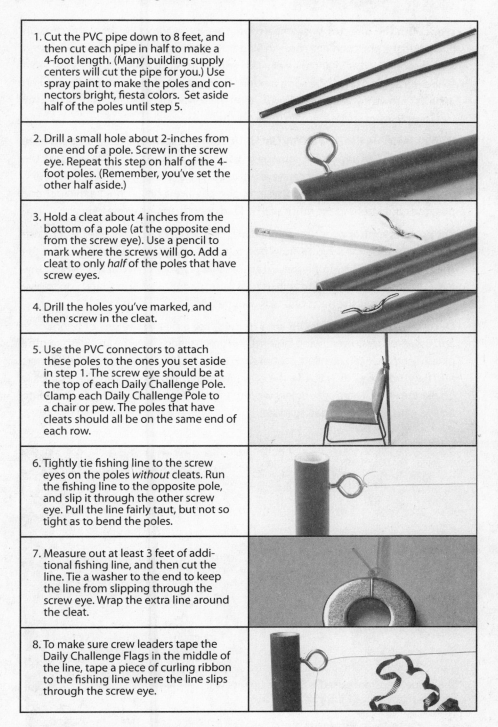

1. Cut the PVC pipe down to 8 feet, and then cut each pipe in half to make a 4-foot length. (Many building supply centers will cut the pipe for you.) Use spray paint to make the poles and connectors bright, fiesta colors. Set aside half of the poles until step 5.

2. Drill a small hole about 2-inches from one end of a pole. Screw in the screw eye. Repeat this step on half of the 4-foot poles. (Remember, you've set the other half aside.)

3. Hold a cleat about 4 inches from the bottom of a pole (at the opposite end from the screw eye). Use a pencil to mark where the screws will go. Add a cleat to only *half* of the poles that have screw eyes.

4. Drill the holes you've marked, and then screw in the cleat.

5. Use the PVC connectors to attach these poles to the ones you set aside in step 1. The screw eye should be at the top of each Daily Challenge Pole. Clamp each Daily Challenge Pole to a chair or pew. The poles that have cleats should all be on the same end of each row.

6. Tightly tie fishing line to the screw eyes on the poles *without* cleats. Run the fishing line to the opposite pole, and slip it through the other screw eye. Pull the line fairly taut, but not so tight as to bend the poles.

7. Measure out at least 3 feet of additional fishing line, and then cut the line. Tie a washer to the end to keep the line from slipping through the screw eye. Wrap the extra line around the cleat.

8. To make sure crew leaders tape the Daily Challenge Flags in the middle of the line, tape a piece of curling ribbon to the fishing line where the line slips through the screw eye.

## For each set of Daily poles, you'll need:

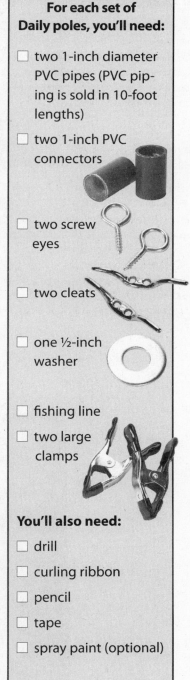

- [ ] two 1-inch diameter PVC pipes (PVC piping is sold in 10-foot lengths)
- [ ] two 1-inch PVC connectors
- [ ] two screw eyes
- [ ] two cleats
- [ ] one ½-inch washer
- [ ] fishing line
- [ ] two large clamps

## You'll also need:

- [ ] drill
- [ ] curling ribbon
- [ ] pencil
- [ ] tape
- [ ] spray paint (optional)

When it's time for Fiesta Crews to add their flags, the person sitting closest to the cleat will unwrap the fishing line and lower the line. When the flags are in place, the same person can pull the line and wrap it around the cleat again!

# Before the Fiesta Begins

## Station Preparation

- **Work with the director to select a room for Sing & Play Olé.** All of the children (including the preschoolers) come to Sing & Play Olé at the same time, so you'll need a large room, such as a sanctuary or a fellowship hall. Since many churches use sanctuaries for singing times, the song motions have been designed to work for children in pews or rows. If you'll be meeting in another room, move the chairs out of the way to allow plenty of space for movement and fun!

- **If you'll be using the *Sing & Play Olé Music* audiocassette or CD, set up a cassette or CD player.** *If at all possible,* arrange to use the church's sound system to play the music. (What an easy way to create an upbeat, almost party-like setting for praising God!) If you can't use the sound system, plan to have a helper hold a microphone near the equipment so the music will be loud enough for everyone to hear.

- **Set up a microphone** (or have your church's sound technician set one up). Practice with the microphone so you'll know how to turn it on and how to remove it from the stand if necessary. A microphone will ensure that *everyone* can hear what you're saying. Even if you're not comfortable using a microphone, we'd encourage you to give it a try. Remember, the microphone is your friend!

- **Decorate the Sing & Play Olé area to look like a fiesta.** Use lots of bright pots and tissue-paper flowers, hang lanterns and green vines, cover the area with colorful piñatas and Mexican blankets, scatter sombreros and maracas, and spread banners and flags from wall to wall. Use the easy directions on page 15 to make your Daily Challenge Poles. There are endless ways to transform your Sing & Play Olé area into an eye-catching, child-pleasing place!

- **You'll need Fiesta Crew signs to show kids where to sit during Sing & Play Olé.** Check with your director to see if the signs will be placed in the room ahead of time. The signs might use numbers or characters, and your director may even color-code each crew. If you need to make crew signs, simply write numbers on colorful poster board, or use the clip art from the *Fiesta! Clip Art, Song Lyrics, and Decorating* CD.

- **Photocopy the Sing & Play Olé sign and arrow from pages 64-65 in this manual, and post the copies along the hallways leading to your room.**

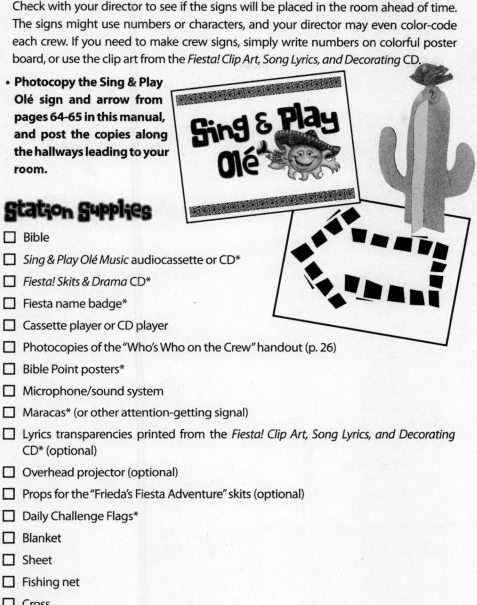

## Station Supplies

- [ ] Bible
- [ ] *Sing & Play Olé Music* audiocassette or CD*
- [ ] *Fiesta! Skits & Drama* CD*
- [ ] Fiesta name badge*
- [ ] Cassette player or CD player
- [ ] Photocopies of the "Who's Who on the Crew" handout (p. 26)
- [ ] Bible Point posters*
- [ ] Microphone/sound system
- [ ] Maracas* (or other attention-getting signal)
- [ ] Lyrics transparencies printed from the *Fiesta! Clip Art, Song Lyrics, and Decorating* CD* (optional)
- [ ] Overhead projector (optional)
- [ ] Props for the "Frieda's Fiesta Adventure" skits (optional)
- [ ] Daily Challenge Flags*
- [ ] Blanket
- [ ] Sheet
- [ ] Fishing net
- [ ] Cross
- [ ] Sunglasses

*available from Group Publishing or your local Group supplier

## Fiesta Safety Tips

Set up your CD player near an electrical outlet so that the children (and you!) won't trip over the cord. If you must stretch cords across the room, use electrical tape or duct tape to fasten them to the floor.

Have children spread out so they don't bump into one another as they do the motions.

**May God bless you as you help kids get fired up about Jesus' love!**

### RED HOT TIPS

*Attention-getting signals let kids know when it's time to stop what they're doing and look at you. You can use the maracas (available from Group Publishing or your local Group supplier) or another signal of your choice. The first time children come to Sing & Play Olé, introduce and rehearse your attention-getting signal. Once the kids are familiar with the signal, regaining their attention will be automatic.*

# DAY 1

Whatever hardships life had dealt the paralyzed man, it's clear that he was blessed with faithful friends. When his friends heard that Jesus was in town, they immediately brought the paralyzed man to see Jesus. Even throngs of people couldn't keep them from laying their friend at Jesus' feet. Believing that Jesus could heal their friend, the men tore away part of a roof so they could lower the man to Jesus. With love and compassion, Jesus forgave the man's sins and healed him completely. What an amazing picture of friendship, devotion, and love this story gives us!

For the kids at your VBS, friendships are a major part of everyday life. Kids crave a friend who will listen, laugh, encourage, and play. They want friendships that are lasting, faithful, and fun. Unfortunately, faithful friends can be hard to find. We've all heard, "I'll be your best friend if…" or "You're not my friend anymore because…"

What a joy and comfort to realize that Jesus is our forever friend! Jesus doesn't put boundaries or conditions on our relationship with him. He is faithful, loving, and caring. Today's activities will help children discover that their dearest friend is Jesus.

 Because  Jesus is our friend, we can

- model the friendship Jesus shows us,

- tell others about him, and

- trust that he will always be with us.

## BIBLE POINT:

Jesus is our friend.

## TREASURE VERSE:

 "Now you are my friends" *(John 15:15)*.

## BIBLE STORY:

**Men bring their friend to Jesus for healing** *(Luke 5:17-25).*

## DAY 1 BIBLE POINT

 Jesus is our friend.

### RED HOT TIPS

*Although we've written "Frieda's Fiesta Adventure" for a woman, you could have a man play the role and change the character's name to Freddy.*

### RED HOT TIPS

*If you're using the Fiesta! Skits & Drama CD for Frieda's lines, have a volunteer pause the CD between each of Frieda's lines. You can speak your line, and then your volunteer can play Frieda's next line.*

# Frieda's Fiesta Adventure (Day 1)

**Bible Point:** Jesus is our friend.

### Props
*Frieda looks every inch the flashy tourist: She wears oversize sunglasses, a sun hat, a brightly colored shirt, and shorts. She has just finished shopping and is carrying two enormous shopping bags overflowing with items such as scarves and tissue paper flowers. During today's skit, she'll need to take cell phone, a colorful tarp, and a candy bar from one of her bags.*

(*Sound effect of a diesel bus as it fires up noisily and pulls away.* **Frieda** *rushes onto the stage from stage right, looking stage left. She's waving her bags and yelling after the departing bus.*)

**Frieda:** Wait! Wait for me! Bus driver! (*Sags with frustration.*) I can't believe the tour bus left me behind! (*Looking around in dismay*) I'm scared. I'm alone. I don't have any friends in this little village.

(**Leader** *enters stage right, notices Frieda, and pauses to watch.*)

**Leader:** Um, excuse me…

(**Frieda** *doesn't hear Leader.*)

**Frieda:** (*Punching numbers into her cell phone.*) Maybe I can still catch them. Hello? Wisconsin on Wheels Tour Company? This is Frieda Johnson from Wackanack, Wisconsin, and you just left me behind in San Anita, Mexico. (*Pauses.*)

Well, I was a little late getting back after shopping…but just two hours. (*Pauses.*)

Can't you please call your bus driver and turn that thing around right now? (*Pauses.*) When will it be back? (*Pauses.*)

Four days? I can't stay here four more days! Where will I sleep? What will I eat? What friends will I talk to? (*Wound up with worry.*) Please, have the bus driver turn around and get me...Hello? Hello? Why, he hung up on me!

**Leader:** Excuse me, but cell phone reception isn't always good because of the mountains surrounding the village. Perhaps you were cut off.

**Frieda:** Well…I tried…who are you?

**Leader:** My name is [Leader's name]. I'm from [Name of your community]. These kids and I are celebrating at Fiesta!

**Frieda:** (*Sadly*) I'm Frieda Johnson from Wackanack, Wisconsin.

**Leader:** So I heard.

**Frieda:** (*Crossing her arms and thinking*) I guess I'll just sit here in the village square. No, by golly, I'll set up camp here! (*Reaches into a shopping bag and pulls out a tarp.*) Say…can you help me unfold this?

**Leader:** (*Helping*) Sure, but why do you have a tarp with you?

**Frieda:** For moments exactly like this. I say to my husband, "Leroy, I need a big purse because you never know when you'll need a tarp." And here's proof! This tarp will work great for a tent.

(**Frieda** does a lot of bumbling and fumbling with the tarp. She covers herself with it and then falls over, her feet flying up in the air. Then her head pops out from underneath. Finally, **Frieda** and **Leader** step back to admire their handiwork—which looks like a jumbled-up tarp.)

**Leader:** Hmmm…well, so much for a tent. What will you eat?

**Frieda:** I have all kinds of goodies in my bags. I'll show you. See?

(Frieda pulls out a candy bar.)

**Leader:** A candy bar? For the next four days?

**Frieda:** (Sadly) I'll just chew slowly. Really, really, really slowly.

**Leader:** Look, you don't have to be lonely. You can hang out with us and be our guest.

**Frieda:** But why are you helping me?

**Leader:** Because it looks like you need a friend. (Motions to kids.) These kids and I are learning that  Jesus is our friend. ("Viva!") You never need to feel alone, because Jesus is with you no matter where you go—no matter if you are in a little village (pointing off stage right) or in Wisconsin. In the meantime, I think you can stay right there.

**Frieda:** Thanks for telling me about Jesus, and thanks for being my friend. I sure do need one. Let's leave my tent set up. We can come back later, and I'll show you how we Johnsons from Wackanack make s'mores. I'll even use my candy bar!

(Frieda exits stage right.)

# Firing Up for Fiesta

Before starting the first day of Fiesta, photocopy the "Who's Who on the Crew" handout on page 26. You'll need one handout for each Fiesta Crew.

Before the children arrive, check to make sure that all of the equipment is set up and working. About 30 minutes before the Fiesta is scheduled to start, begin playing the *Sing & Play Olé Music* CD. This will create a fun and inviting atmosphere as the kids and crew leaders enter your area for the first time. Continue the music until you're ready to begin the program.

*On Day 1 only*, the preschoolers will go straight to the Silly Chilies area instead of attending Sing & Play Olé. On the first day of a busy week, the younger children will benefit from orientation time with their leaders.

When you're ready to begin, introduce yourself, and **SAY: Welcome to Fiesta—where kids are fired up about Jesus!** Ask kids to shout, "We're fired up about Jesus!" as they crouch low and then jump up high. **Each day at our Fiesta, we'll begin Sing & Play Olé by singing fun songs and doing motions with the songs. A fiesta is a party and a celebration. We're celebrating because we're fired up about our friend Jesus!**

**Before we start, get to know the people in your Fiesta Crew a bit. Take turns telling one another your name and what's your favorite thing to do at a party.**

**RED HOT TIPS**

*To save time, you may want to make photocopies of the "Who's Who on the Crew?" handout (p. 26) several days ahead of time. Then make sure a copy is in each Crew Bag to eliminate the need to distribute the handouts during the first Sing & Play Olé session.*

**RED HOT TIPS**

*Check with your VBS director to find out what time you should start singing. For example, if your program begins at 8:30, you may want to start singing warm-up songs with the children at 8:20. If you're planning to take song requests from kids, you may want to begin even earlier.*

# DAY 1

**RED HOT TIPS**

*The motions to the songs are very simple. Introduce new songs quickly. The children pick up the words and motions as they sing!*

**FIESTA FINDINGS**

*When kids sang "Never Be the Same!" in the field test, they were awesome! The voices, laughter, and music definitely brought a fiesta feel to our room. Throughout the week, kids kept asking to do the "cha-cha song."*

As an example, tell kids your name and something you like to do, such as listen to music or talk with friends. Then allow a few moments for the kids in the Fiesta Crews to get to know one another and their crew leader.

After two minutes, sound your maracas or other attention-getting device. Help kids practice listening for the maraca sound and focusing their attention on the leader when they hear it.

**SAY:** During each Fiesta day, you'll experience a Bible Point and a Bible story. Today's Bible Point is [H] Jesus is our friend. Every time you hear someone say today's Bible Point, [H] Jesus is our friend, during our Fiesta vacation Bible school, I want you to throw both of your hands in the air to make a V shape as you shout, "Viva!"

Show kids how to do the sign (see photo).

**SAY:** Let's practice. [H] Jesus is our friend! Lead kids in doing the sign and shouting "Viva!" **The reason we say "Viva" is because *Viva* means life. We live now and we'll live forever because of Jesus!**

"Viva!"

**During this week's Fiesta, we're going to have fun learning about Jesus' love. Let's start with our theme song, "Never Be the Same!" Sing loud, because we want everyone to hear about our friend Jesus.**

**CD Track 1** Before leading "Never Be the Same!" briefly explain the motions. See page 52 for the words and motions. Show kids how to face one direction with their hands on the shoulders of kids in front of them when they sing the first two "cha cha" lines. Then have kids switch directions to face the other way for the second half of the "cha cha" part.

After the song, **SAY:** Great singing! Our theme song will help us remember today's Bible Point, [H] Jesus is our friend. ("Viva!") Hmm…is there a Bible Memory Buddy that can help us remember the Bible Point? I know! Bring out the poster of Ray, and ask a volunteer to hold it. **This is our friend Ray. Look! He's a smiling, friendly sun. All animals, plants, and humans on earth need the sun so they can live and grow! Just as we need Jesus so we can live and grow. When I feel sunshine on me, I feel happy and warm all over. That's how I feel with my friend Jesus.**

Cha-cha!

**Our friend Ray, who makes us feel happy and warm all over, will help us remember today's Bible Point, [H] Jesus is our friend!** ("Viva!")

Bring out your Bible, and **SAY:** The Bible is full of priceless treasures because it's God's Word. Each day at Fiesta, we will discover a Treasure Verse from the Bible. Today's Treasure Verse from the Bible is found in John 15:15. The Treasure Verse says, "Now you are my friends." These are *Jesus'* words to us. Jesus is calling *us* his friends. Let's do some motions to help us remember our Treasure Verse. Have the kids follow your motions as you raise your arms and look up (because it's Jesus saying the verse), point around the room, and then hug one person.

"Now              you are              my friends."

**We have a friend in Jesus! He loves us so! Let's sing a song with those same words: "What a Friend We Have in Jesus."**

**CD Track 2** Briefly go over the words and motions to "No, Not One/What a Friend We Have in Jesus." Show the kids the motion for *struggle*. Ask them to point their pointer fingers toward each other horizontally and then move their arms side to side. The words and motions are on page 53. Encourage the volunteer to stay up front and help lead the song.

After the song, **SAY:** Jesus is our friend. ("Viva!") **Today you'll learn about a man whose good friends brought him to Jesus for healing. The man couldn't walk, so his friends carried him on a mat!** Ask another volunteer to stand up front and hold the blanket. **The men knew that** Jesus is our friend ("Viva!").

"Struggle"

**There were crowds of people around Jesus, and the men couldn't get through.** Have everyone look around the room. **We have a crowd of people here at Fiesta! The men had to find a way to get their friend through a crowd of people to see Jesus. So they put their friend on a mat** (motion to the volunteer who's holding the blanket) **and lowered him down to Jesus through the roof! What good friends!**

**Let's sing another song about Jesus' friendship. It's called "I Have a Friend" or "Yo Tengo un Amigo." The song uses English words and Spanish words to say the same thing. Listen to the CD, and sing along. You'll get it!**

**CD Track 3** Briefly review the motions and then lead the kids in singing "I Have a Friend." To show kids the motion for *friend*, hook your two pointer fingers together. The words and motions are on page 54.

"Friend"

# DAY 1

*During our field test, the Sing & Play Olé Leader wondered if she should teach the Spanish or let the CD do the teaching. She decided to let the kids just sing along and learn as they sang—and they did! This song was another huge favorite during our field test week.*

*Kids had great fun with "Yo Tengo un Amigo." By the end of the week, everyone was shouting "Olé!" on the last two beats of the song. We rattled the roof!*

*"Are you sure you want to leave all those kids with only one leader?" Don't worry about kids misbehaving while their Fiesta Crew Leaders are away. In our field test, the kids were having too much fun singing to notice that their leaders were gone! Plus knowing that their leaders were praying for them communicated a real message of love.*

After the song, **SAY: Great singing! You're going to get to know some fun friends this week. Every Fiesta Crew has a leader who guides the adventure and makes sure all is well. Your crew leaders are an important part of Fiesta this week. Each day, they'll meet just outside the Sing & Play Olé area for a quick huddle and a prayer.**

**Fiesta Crew Leaders, while we sing a song or two, head on out to meet with our Fiesta Director for a brief huddle and a prayer right now. Then come join us again for more fun.**

**I'm glad that**  **Jesus is our friend.** ("Viva!") **On the count of three, all together shout, "Jesus is our friend," and I'll say, "Viva!" Ready? One, two, three…**

Have the kids shout, "Jesus is our friend!" Then shout an enthusiastic "Viva!"

**SAY: Let's sing a song that says we love our friend Jesus so much that we want everyone to know about him.**

Quickly show kids the motions, and then lead them in singing "We Want to See Jesus Lifted High." The words and motions are on page 55. Encourage the children to sing loudly so the crew leaders will be serenaded as they come back from their huddle and prayer.

After the song, **SAY: What a great song! We want everyone to know that**  **Jesus is our friend!** ("Viva!") **Jesus is the only way to heaven.**

Ask the kids to sit down. **SAY: It takes a lot of people to make a fiesta a success. All jobs are important. At Fiesta this week, every Fiesta Crew member has an important job, too. There are Readers, Fiesta Guides, Materials Managers, Coaches, and Prayer People.** Have a few volunteers help you distribute the "Who's Who on the Crew" handouts if you haven't already put the handouts in the Crew Bags.

**I'll read all of the job descriptions aloud. Everyone listen and think about which job you'd like to do. Then your Fiesta Crew Leaders will go over the job descriptions with you as you decide who in your crew will do each job.**

Read the following job descriptions aloud to the group.

### Reader

- likes to read
- reads Bible passages aloud

### Fiesta Guide

- chooses action ideas for traveling through Fiesta (such as tiptoeing, hopping, galloping, or marching)
- helps monitor the daily schedule to let the crew know what's coming next

### Materials Manager

- likes to collect and distribute supplies
- helps carry the crew's finished crafts and other goodies in the Crew Bag
- helps attach the Daily Challenge Flags

### Coach

**Coach**

- likes to smile and make people happy
- makes sure people use kind words and actions
- leads crew in cheering during games

**Prayer Person**

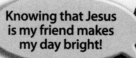

Knowing that Jesus is my friend makes my day bright!

- likes to pray and isn't afraid to pray aloud
- makes sure the crew takes time to pray each day
- leads or opens prayer times

After you've read through the job descriptions, **SAY:** Fiesta **Crew Leaders, it's time to help the kids in your crew choose their jobs. The jobs are listed on your name tags. A crew member can have a different job each day or the same job for the entire week. And this would be a good time for all of you to make sure you know the name of everyone else in your crew. So, kids, when you've decided who will do what job in your crew, you each can say your name and the job you'll do today.**

Allow a few minutes for kids to choose the jobs. Circulate among the crews, and offer help and encouragement as needed. If a Fiesta Crew has fewer than five children, let one child have two jobs. If a crew has more than five children, it's fine to give the same job to two or three kids.

**SAY: You all have important jobs now. The fun and enthusiasm you bring to these jobs will help us have an awesome week here at Fiesta. Now, let's close with a special prayer. When I say the name of a job, everyone with that job stand while I pray for you. When I call the next job, you can sit down. Ready?**

**Fiesta Guides.** Pause for kids to stand. Then pray: **Dear God, thank you for these Fiesta Guides. Help them as they guide their crews and manage the daily schedule. In Jesus' name, amen.**

**Coaches.** Pause for kids to stand. Then pray: **Dear God, thank you for these Coaches. Help them be good encouragers who build up the other members of their crew. In Jesus' name, amen.**

**Materials Managers.** Pause for kids to stand. Then pray: **Dear God, thank you for these Materials Managers. Help them be good servants as they collect and distribute important supplies. In Jesus' name, amen.**

**Readers.** Pause for kids to stand. Then pray: **Dear God, thank you for these Readers. Help them read your Word and share it with the crews. In Jesus' name, amen.**

**Prayer People.** Pause for kids to stand. Then pray: **Dear God, thank you for these Prayer People. Help them know just what to say when they speak to you. In Jesus' name, amen.**

**Fiesta Crew Leaders and assistant crew leaders.** Pause for them to stand, and then pray: **Dear God, thank you for these crew leaders and assistant leaders. Help them to be wise leaders as they guide the children at Fiesta. In Jesus' name, amen.**

Have the Fiesta Crew Leaders and assistant crew leaders sit down, and then **SAY: Now our Fiesta Director will give us some special instructions. Listen carefully, and then your Fiesta Crew can visit all the exciting stations!**

Introduce the director. He or she will make announcements, remind Fiesta Crews which group they're in, pray, and dismiss kids to their stations.

**RED HOT TIPS**

*Knowing kids' names and calling children by their names is an important part of creating a warm and affirming environment. Be sure to give plenty of opportunities each day for crews to make this simple but meaningful connection.*

**RED HOT TIPS**

*At the end of each day's Sing & Play Olé, you'll be free to help the VBS director until it's time for Fiesta Finale. You can offer to run errands, check in with other station leaders, or even fill in as a Fiesta Crew Leader in a pinch. Your director will appreciate your help!*

# Who's Who on the Crew

**Reader**

- likes to read
- reads Bible passages aloud

**Fiesta Guide**

- likes to help others
- chooses action ideas for traveling through Fiesta (such as tiptoeing, hopping, galloping, or marching)
- helps monitor the daily schedule to let the crew know what's coming next

**Materials Manager**

- likes to distribute and collect supplies
- helps carry the crew's bag
- helps attach the Daily Challenge Flags

**Coach**

- likes to smile and make people happy
- makes sure people use kind words and actions
- leads group in cheering during games

**Prayer Person**

- likes to pray and isn't afraid to pray aloud
- makes sure the crew takes time to pray each day
- leads or opens prayer times

# DAY 2

To his followers, Jesus really was life. Followers, including Mary and Martha, believed that Jesus was God's Son. They were faithfully committed to following and obeying Jesus. They had faith that Jesus could do anything. So imagine their dismay when Jesus didn't hurry to Lazarus' bedside. Instead, Mary and Martha watched their brother die while Jesus remained a few miles away. But Jesus took their grief and turned it to amazement as he called Lazarus from the tomb. He had been dead four days, but Lazarus arose and walked from the tomb. Where there was pain and death, Jesus created joy and life.

Even kids who know Jesus might hesitate to say that Jesus is their life. For kids today, life usually revolves around sports, school, clubs, and friends. Jesus might be part of their lives, but he's not the most important part. That's why it's important that we demonstrate what it means to make Jesus the focal point of everyday life.

Jesus not only promises eternal life but also gives us a reason for living each day. Use the activities in today's lesson to help kids discover what it means to make Jesus the most important part of our lives.

 Because 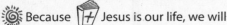 Jesus is our life, we will

- show our love for Jesus in all we do,

- praise God for giving us the gift of Jesus, and

- find ways to help others know Jesus.

## BIBLE POINT:

 Jesus is our life.

## TREASURE VERSE:

 "And you must love the Lord your God with all your heart" (Deuteronomy 6:5).

## BIBLE STORY:

Jesus raises Lazarus from the dead (John 11).

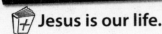

As the kids arrive each day, have the Fiesta Crew Leaders remind them of their jobs. If the crews receive new children, or if the kids want to trade jobs each day, Fiesta Crew Leaders can reassign the jobs and remind the children of their duties.

# Frieda's Fiesta Adventure (Day 2)

**Bible Point:**  **Jesus is our life**

> **Props**
> *Frieda wears her Day 1 costume and carries her two big, stuffed shopping bags. She'll need a pot of flowers and a large jug for collecting water. Place the jug on the floor at center stage. The Leader will need a towel.*

*(**Leader** enters stage left. **Frieda** enters stage right, struggling to hold her shopping bags and her pot of flowers.)*

**Leader:** *Hola!* Where have you been, my friend Frieda?

**Frieda:** I've been shopping in your cool little village. Shopping is my life! I don't think I could live a single day without shopping.

**Leader:** Wow! When you say something is your life, you mean that it's very important to you.

**Frieda:** Yes! How did you know? Shopping is number one in my life. It is *verrrry* important to me. When I think about a day without shopping, I think it must be like a day without M&M's candies or a day without sunshine.

**Leader:** Wow. You really *do* mean shopping is your life. It looks like you've shopped for a lot of interesting things.

**Frieda:** I have lots of lovely items in my shopping bags. And look at these lovely flowers I bought. *(Holds the pot of flowers high.)* I need to get water for these flowers, though. Flowers need water to live, and this pot they're in is very dry. *(Pauses while looking around.)* Oh, look! Here's a jug I can use to go collect water from the fountain in the yard. *(Holds onto her shopping treasures as she tries to balance the jug on her head.)* I'll just slip outside and be right back.

**Leader:** Hurry back to tell me more about your morning!

*(**Frieda** hurries off stage right as she struggles with her load. **Leader** begins to talk with the kids. All of a sudden, we hear a crash and a splash. Then **Frieda** enters stage right, empty-handed and wet.)*

**Leader:** Frieda! What happened?

**Frieda:** I was hanging on to all the things I bought that were so important to me. I tried to get water for the flowers, but everything went wrong. Before I knew it, I lost all my shopping items and my flowers, and I was covered from head to foot with water!

**Leader:** As your new friend, I have to tell you something important.

**Frieda:** What? That you have a towel for me to dry off with? That would be important.

**Leader:** Yes, I have a towel for you to dry off with. *(Hands Frieda a towel.)* But what's most important is that  Jesus is our life. Nothing else should be number one with us—not shopping, not flowers, not anything—just Jesus. He loves us so much that he died for our sins.

**Frieda:** I just get so sidetracked with other things. Then those other things—like shopping—take up so much time in my life. Jesus should be number one in our lives. Maybe you guys could sing some songs about Jesus while I get into some dry clothes.

# Firing Up for Fiesta

Before the kids arrive, check to make sure that all of the equipment is set up and working. About 15 minutes before your VBS is scheduled to start, begin playing the *Sing & Play Olé Music* CD to create a fun and inviting atmosphere as kids enter your area and gather in their Fiesta Crews.

After the kids have arrived, **SAY: Welcome back to another day at Fiesta—where kids are fired up about Jesus.** Ask kids to shout, "We're fired up about Jesus!" as they crouch low and then jump up high.

**Let's sing a song right away so everyone hears us and knows our fantastic Fiesta is beginning!**

 Lead the kids in singing "Never Be the Same!" The words and motions are on page 52.

After the song, **SAY: Great singing! All week long, we're going to learn about Jesus. Let's learn another song and tell Jesus how much we love him. We'll clap, shout, and stamp our feet to show Jesus how much we love him. The song is called "I'm Gonna Clap My Hands."**

 Lead the kids in singing "I'm Gonna Clap My Hands." The words and motions are on page 60.

**SAY: Yesterday was so much fun at our Fiesta because we learned that  Jesus is our friend!** ("Viva!") **In just a minute, I want you to talk in your crews about what you did for your Daily Challenges. How did you show others that Jesus is our friend?** ("Viva!") **I showed others that Jesus is our friend.** ("Viva!") **Tell about something you did to show others that Jesus is your friend. For example, you might say that you helped a neighbor with an outdoor chore.**

Hold up a Daily Challenge Flag. **SAY: Crew leaders, take out the Daily Challenge Flag from your Crew Bag. Crew members, take turns telling your crew how you showed others that Jesus is our friend.** ("Viva!")

After a minute, walk among the children with the microphone, and let several children tell about ways they showed others that Jesus is their friend.

**SAY: Great ways to show others that Jesus is our friend!** ("Viva!") **Now, we're going to lower the lines of our Daily Challenge Poles. The Materials Manager from your crew will tape the Daily Challenge Flag to the line. We'll sing a song and raise the flags high to show others that we know Jesus is our friend!** ("Viva!"). **By the end of the week, we'll see lots of flags waving above. We're so fired up about Jesus that we want *everyone* to be fired up about him.**

**Let's sing "We Want to See Jesus Lifted High."**

## FIESTA FINDINGS

On the last three beats of "Never Be the Same!" we shouted "cha cha cha" as we punched our fists in the air. It was fun! Kids really got into it.

## FIESTA FINDINGS

The VBS director led the sharing time during the field test. Lots of children all over the room wanted to share, so the director was careful to choose volunteers from the back and sides of the room, as well as from the front. One child prayed with a friend who was sad, and another child sang a VBS song to her grandma!

**Hanging Daily Challenge flags**

## FIESTA FINDINGS

*It was so exciting to see the first Daily Challenge Flags raised high. Singing the song as we raised the flags gave us goose bumps! We could just anticipate what the Sing & Play Olé area would look like by the end of the week. For the children, the flags were a great visual reminder of how they were spreading Jesus' love all around their homes, neighborhoods, and community.*

Sing "We Want to See Jesus Lifted High," and watch the Daily Challenge Flags go up! **Track 4**

After the song, **SAY:** I can't wait to see our Daily Challenge Flags multiply throughout the week! We want everyone to be fired up about Jesus! Hold up a Bible. **God's Word—the Bible—encourages us to tell everyone about Jesus!**

Today at our Fiesta, we'll learn that **Jesus is our life. So whenever you hear someone say, "Jesus is our life," shout, "Viva!"** Practice saying the Bible Point a few times so that kids can show you the Viva sign as they shout "Viva!"

**We need a Bible Memory Buddy to help us remember today's Bible Point. Who remembers the Bible Memory Buddy from yesterday?** Ask a volunteer to hold the picture of Ray, and have kids say yesterday's Bible Point: "Jesus is our friend." ("Viva!") Ask another child to hold the blanket and briefly say what he or she learned about the men who brought their friend to Jesus for healing.

**Hmmm…I wonder what Bible Memory Buddy could help us remember that Jesus is our life.** ("Viva!") **I know! Rosa!** Ask a volunteer to hold up a poster of Rosa. **How do jack rabbits move around?** Encourage kids to jump up and down. **Jack rabbits have strong muscles in their legs that help them jump up and down. Rosa is a jumping jack rabbit! She jumps around with happiness because Jesus is our life.** ("Viva!") **Rosa will also help us remember today's Bible story.**

**I need one more volunteer to help me.** Choose a volunteer, and wrap a sheet around him or her. **Our Bible story tells about Jesus raising Lazarus from the dead. When a person died in those days, people wrapped the person with cloth. You'll have to wait until Hot Bible Adventures to hear the rest of the story!**

Bring out your Bible, and **SAY:** The Bible tells us that Jesus should be the most important thing to us. **Jesus is our life!** ("Viva!") **Today's Treasure Verse from the Bible is found in Deuteronomy 6:5. The Treasure Verse says, "And you must love the Lord your God with all your heart."** Point to someone on "you," cross your arms in front of you and twist back and forth like you're giving a big squeeze on "love the Lord your God." Pat both hands on your chest on each word of "all your heart."

> Don't you want to jump for joy because Jesus is your life?

**"And you must**      **love the Lord your God**      **with all your heart."**

**CD** Track 5 — **While our leaders go out for a huddle and a prayer, let's sing a song called "I Got the Joy." Jesus gives us so much joy that we want to sing, clap, jump, and shout! We've got the joy of the Lord in our hearts because [image] Jesus is our life!** ("Viva!")

**CD** Track 7 — Briefly teach the children the motions. Lead the kids in singing "I've Got the Joy." The words and motions are on page 56.

After the song, **SAY: I loved your singing! Let's sing another song to remind us that Jesus raised Lazarus from the dead. People were sad because Lazarus was sick for several days and then he died. Jesus came and raised him to life after he died! Let's sing "Trading My Sorrows."**

Briefly review the motions. Show kids how to do a thumbs-up motion on "yes" and then form an L with their pointer fingers and thumbs for "Lord." Lead the kids in singing "Trading My Sorrows." The words and motions are on page 59.

**RED HOT TIPS**

*Each day your director might want to tell jokes that go along with the day's Bible Buddy. Even though the jokes are corny, the kids will love them and may even make up a few of their own!*

"Yes,

Lord."

After the song, **SAY: We say "Yes, Lord," to Jesus, because [image] Jesus is our life!** ("Viva!") **Now let's welcome our Fiesta Director who will prepare us for another exciting day.**

Introduce the director who will make announcements, close in prayer, and dismiss the kids to their stations. Play the *Sing & Play Olé Music* CD as the children leave the Sing & Play Olé area.

# DAY 3

As Jesus began his ministry on earth, he sought faithful friends who would spread the life-changing message of God's love and forgiveness. Walking beside the Sea of Galilee, Jesus spied two fishermen—the brothers Simon Peter and Andrew. He called to them, "Come, follow me, and I will show you how to fish for people!" Perhaps they'd heard Jesus' preaching or seen the kindness in his eyes. Or maybe it was just something in his voice that touched a need deep in their hearts. Without hesitation, the brothers dropped their nets, left the only profession they knew, and followed Jesus.

Nearby, James and John were fishing with their father. Jesus called out to them, too. Scripture doesn't tell us how much these brothers knew about Jesus. Did they believe he was God's Son? Did they trust that he truly was the Messiah? In any case, the brothers immediately left the boat, left their family, and followed Jesus. It was that simple.

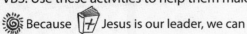

For kids today, the decision to follow Jesus may not feel so simple. In some circles, it's not cool to be a Christian. Friends may laugh. And following Jesus means *not* following what other kids might do. That's why the activities in today's lesson are designed to help kids verbalize and practice ways they'll follow God in everyday life. God has big plans for the kids at your VBS! Use these activities to help them make Jesus their leader each day.

Because  Jesus is our leader, we can

- choose to do things God's way,

- show our friends what it means to follow Jesus, and

- believe that we're doing what is right.

## BIBLE POINT:

 **Jesus is our leader.**

## TREASURE VERSE:

**"Jesus called out to them, 'Come, follow me'"** *(Matthew 4:19).*

## BIBLE STORY:

**Jesus chooses his first disciples** *(Matthew 4:18-22).*

## DAY 3 BIBLE POINT

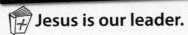 Jesus is our leader.

# Frieda's Fiesta Adventure (Day 3)

**Bible Point:** Jesus is our leader.

> **Props**
> *Frieda wears her usual attire. Sprinkle water on her face so she looks like she's sweating.*

*(Leader stands stage left, and Frieda runs in from stage right. She's exhausted. She places both hands on her knees as she breathes deeply in and out. Finally, Frieda lies on the floor.)*

**Leader:** Frieda! What happened to you?

**Frieda:** Well…*(panting)* I love this little village so much. *(Pants some more.)* I thought I'd be sad and alone when I was left here at the beginning of the week. *(Pants some more.)* But I thought…NO! *(Gets up on her hands and knees.)* By golly! *(Gets up on her knees.)* I'm going to make the most of my stay. *(Stands all the way up, and then drops back down to the floor.)*

**Leader:** What happened?

**Frieda:** Well, I hired a tour guide to be my leader. *(Takes deep breaths.)* I asked him to give me a tour of this village, San Anita. *(Takes more deep breaths.)*

**Leader:** That sounds good. You hired a tour guide to be your leader.

**Frieda:** Yes…it sounds good. BUT…he thought I asked for a tour of San Bonita, which is a village 10 miles from here. *(Takes more deep breaths as she tries to sit up.)* My tour guide led me on a 20-mile jog—10 miles there and 10 miles back! *(Frieda falls back on the floor.)*

**Leader:** Well, I'm sure your tour guide meant well, even though he didn't hear well. I know someone who *always* leads us in the right direction.

**Frieda:** *(Sits up.)* Who? *(Lies back down.)*

**Leader:** Jesus is our leader. ("Viva!") He wants us to follow his ways in life, and we'll always go the right direction. Today at Fiesta, we'll learn about Jesus calling the first disciples who followed him.

*(Leader grabs Frieda and drags her off stage right.)* Let's go get you a drink of water so you can learn about the disciples who knew Jesus was the best leader of all.

# Firing Up for Fiesta

Before kids arrive, check to make sure that all of the equipment is set up and working. About 15 minutes before your VBS is scheduled to start, begin playing the *Sing & Play Olé Music* CD to create a fun and inviting atmosphere as kids enter your area and gather in their Fiesta Crews.

## FIESTA FINDINGS

*We all started looking forward to the Daily Challenge reports. Kids showed others that Jesus is their life by saying prayers with their family and reading the Treasure Verse from their Bible at home!*

**SAY: Welcome to Day 3 of Fiesta—where kids are fired up about Jesus.** Ask kids to shout, "We're fired up about Jesus!" as they crouch low and then jump high. **Let's sing "Never Be the Same!" so everyone knows our Fiesta is beginning!**

**CD Track 1** Lead "Never Be the Same!" The words and motions are on page 52.

**SAY: Great singing! Yesterday we learned that Jesus is our leader.** ("Viva!") **In just a minute, I want you to talk in your crews about what you did for your Daily Challenges. How did you show others that Jesus is our life?** ("Viva!") Relate a personal example, such as that you wore a Christian T-shirt to the grocery store and told a clerk about Jesus.

Hold up a Daily Challenge Flag. **SAY: Take out the Daily Challenge Flag from your Crew Bag. Then, crew members, take turns telling your crew how you showed others that Jesus is our life.** ("Viva!")

After a minute, walk around with the microphone, and let several children tell about ways they showed others that Jesus is their life.

**SAY: Great ways to show others that Jesus is our life!** ("Viva!") **Now, we're going to lower the lines of our Daily Challenge Poles. The Materials Manager from your crew will tape the Daily Challenge Flag to the line. We'll sing a song and raise the flags high to show others that we know that Jesus is our life!** ("Viva!"). **By the end of the week, we'll see lots of flags waving above. We're so fired up about Jesus that we want *everyone* to be fired up about him. Let's sing "We Want to See Jesus Lifted High."**

**CD Track 4** Sing "We Want to See Jesus Lifted High," and watch the flags go up!

**At today's Fiesta, we'll learn that Jesus is our leader.** ("Viva!") **We need a Bible Memory Buddy to help us remember today's Bible Point. But first, who remembers the Bible Memory Buddy from the first day's Fiesta?** Ask a volunteer to hold the picture of Ray, and have kids say that day's Bible Point: Jesus is our friend. ("Viva!") Ask another volunteer to hold the blanket close by Ray, and ask the kids what they learned. **We learned about the men who took their friend on a mat to Jesus for healing.**

**Who remembers the Bible Memory Buddy from yesterday?** Ask a volunteer to hold up a poster of Rosa, and have kids say yesterday's Bible Point: Jesus is our life. ("Viva!") Ask a child to wrap up in the sheet, and ask kids what they learned. **We learned about Jesus raising Lazarus from the dead.**

**Today's Bible Point is Jesus is our leader.** ("Viva!") **I know! Cody the coyote can be our day's Bible Memory Buddy.** Ask a volunteer to hold up the Cody poster. **Look at Cody. He's a coyote. Some coyotes follow a leader in their pack. Today's Bible story is about some fishermen who decided to follow Jesus, their leader.** Ask a volunteer to stand in front and hold a fishing net. **When Jesus told the fishermen to follow him**

Howl-l-l-l-l you show others that Jesus is your leader?

## FIESTA FINDINGS

and learn about God, who loves the world so much, **they dropped their fishing nets** (have the volunteer drop the fishing net), **left their fishing boats, and followed Jesus. The disciples knew that** Jesus is our leader. ("Viva!")

**Volunteers, stand up here and help me sing a song called "King Jesus Is All." When Jesus calls us, we'll answer and follow him because** Jesus is our leader. ("Viva!")

**Track 6** Before you lead "King Jesus Is All," teach the motions. Show kids the motion for "all" by making a scooping motion with one hand and laying the back of that hand in the palm of the other hand. The words and motions are on page 58.

Bring out your Bible, and **SAY:** The Bible says that Jesus is our leader. ("Viva!") **Today's Treasure Verse from the Bible is found in Matthew 4:19. The Treasure Verse says, "Jesus called out to them, 'Come, follow me.'"** Ask kids to follow you with the Treasure Verse motions. Cup your hands around your mouth when you say, **"Jesus called out to them."** Motion "come here" when you say, "Come, follow me."

**"Jesus called out to them,          'Come, follow me.'"**

**SAY:** It's time for our Fiesta Crew Leaders to go out for a huddle and a prayer. While they're praying for us, let's learn a new song called "Help Me, Jesus." Jesus helps us follow him because  Jesus is our leader. ("Viva!")

Lead "Help Me, Jesus." Briefly show kids the motion for "help" by placing a fist on your open palm and lifting it up. The words and motions are on page 63.

*CD Track 10*

After the song, **SAY:** All our lives, we want to follow Jesus and help others follow him, too. Let's welcome our Fiesta Director who will help us prepare for today.

Introduce the director who will make announcements, pray, and dismiss the kids to their stations. Play the *Sing & Play Olé Music* CD as the children leave the Sing & Play Olé area.

**FIESTA FINDINGS**

*Our VBS director closed each Sing & Play Olé session by inviting a different Prayer Person to pray. This is a super time to reinforce kids' roles and to encourage the children to pray. (And you'd be surprised at the precious prayers kids offered—even preschoolers!)*

# DAY 4

Read John 19:17–20:29 in a translation that's unfamiliar to you so that it seems fresh and new. As you read, put yourself in the place of one of Jesus' disciples. Four days earlier, all of Jerusalem had acclaimed Jesus the promised son of David. But as the week passed, the mood in the city changed from jubilant to ominous. Jesus' enemies started false rumors and influenced the crowds against him. Jesus himself grew quiet and sad. When one of the disciples betrayed Jesus, horror upon horror followed. In history's darkest moment, Jesus died a cruel death—a death on a cross.

For all who loved him, Jesus' death was both unbelievable and undeniable. But it wasn't the end! With morning's dawn came the glorious news that the tomb was empty. Jesus had defeated death. Jesus was alive!

Children today might not have a clear understanding of what a savior is. Perhaps they've seen people saved from impending danger on the news or read comics about a superhero who leaps in to save the day. This is a wonderful opportunity to help kids discover that Jesus saved us from the ultimate danger—an

eternity separated from God. Today's activities are designed to help kids explore how Jesus died so we could have eternal life. Use this lesson to guide kids in understanding that Jesus is their risen Savior.

Because  Jesus is our Savior, we can

- thank and praise God,
- celebrate the hope of eternal life, and
- live in a way that pleases God.

## TREASURE VERSE:

"Since I live, you also will live" (John 14:19).

## BIBLE STORY:

**Jesus dies and rises again** *(John 19:17–20:29).*

## DAY 4 BIBLE POINT

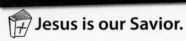 Jesus is our Savior.

# Frieda's Fiesta Adventure (Day 4)

**Bible Point:** 📖 Jesus is our Savior.

> **Props**
> *Frieda wears her usual outfit and carries a large dog collar. The "collar" can be a belt hitched on the last hole. Make the collar look huge. Attach a construction-paper circle "tag" that says "Marko."*

*(Leader stands stage left, and Frieda runs in from stage right. Frieda holds the large dog collar. Play sound effect of a dog barking softly in the background, as if at a distance.)*

**Frieda:** Thank goodness you're here. I have to tell you what's happening to me. *(Waves her hands around as she's telling the story and mimes the actions.)* I walked to the market this morning because I was looking for a fruit stand. We Johnsons from Wackanack, Wisconsin, make a *great* fruit salad. I wanted to make a fruit salad for all of you because you have been such good friends to me throughout the Fiesta week. Well…I looked to my left…to my right…nothing. There wasn't one fruit stand in the whole market! All I saw was this empty dog collar on the ground. *(Holds up the collar.)*

**Leader:** Then what happened?

**Frieda:** *(Still miming all actions)* Then I saw this one man carrying a leash. I thought he was trying to get my attention so I walked over to him and waved the collar as I shouted, "Señor, I am Frieda Johnson from Wackanack, Wisconsin, and I'd like two pounds of peaches." That's when all these people started yelling. I looked around the market to see lots of people waving, so I waved back. "Hi, there! It's been fun visiting your village." *(The dog's barking gets louder.)*

**Leader:** *Then* what happened?

**Frieda:** Then I saw they weren't waving. They were *pointing*. Pointing right *behind* me at a dog. A *big* dog. A big dog with sharp, pointy teeth and a *really* bad attitude.

**Leader:** Were you scared?

**Frieda:** Well, *(pointing a thumb at her chest)* back in Wackanack, Wisconsin, I owned dogs, and I knew *exactly* what to do.

**Leader:** And?

**Frieda:** I planted my feet and put my hands on my hips.

**Leader:** And?

**Frieda:** *(Leaning forward and squinting.)* And I looked the dog square in the eye.

**Leader:** And?

**Frieda:** And I shouted, "Sit!"

**Leader:** And?

**Frieda:** The dog sat at first. But the man with the leash—he must've been the dog's owner—came running at the dog, and the dog started chasing me! *(Demonstrates by running wildly around in a circle a few times, waving her arms and screaming.)* And I didn't slow down until I was back here. *(Sound effect of the dog barking loudly)*

**Leader:** Wait a minute! Take a deep breath!

*(**Leader** grabs the collar from Frieda and throws it off stage right. Shouts.)* Señor! Here's your dog's collar! Go ahead and grab him with the leash! *(Sound effect dog slurping and happy panting)*

**Frieda:** You saved me.

**Leader:** I just guessed the owner needed the dog's collar so he could tie him up. You're OK now. You know who really saves us?

**Frieda:** Well, from what I've been learning all week at Fiesta, I'll make a guess that Jesus is our Savior. ("Viva!")

**Leader:** You're right! Jesus saves us from our sins. Jesus died and rose again so we could live with him forever in heaven. Jesus saves us from a lot more than a big, barking dog!

*(Sound effect of Frieda's cell phone ringing)*

**Frieda:** Hello? Oh, hi, honey. *(Covers the phone and talks to the Leader.)* It's my husband. *(Talks into cell phone.)* Yes, still here in San Anita. *(Pauses.)* No, I'm OK. In fact, it's been *bueno—muy bueno.* I'm staying with some friends who are having a fiesta. They've been telling me about the Savior, Jesus. I'll explain when I get home. OK, honey. Love you. Hey, when you feed the dog tonight, make sure his collar is on tight. *(Pauses.)* Well, just because…*Trust* me on this. Bye-bye.

**Leader:** Are you ready to go home?

**Frieda:** Yes, but before I go I want you to tell me more about our Savior, Jesus. Can you tell me while I pack?

**Leader:** I *love* telling people about Jesus. He's my Savior! Let's sing a song first.

*(Frieda joins kids for a song, and then exits stage right.)*

## Firing Up for Fiesta

Before the kids arrive, check to make sure that all of the equipment is set up and working. About 15 minutes before your VBS is scheduled to start, begin playing the *Sing & Play Olé Music* CD. The songs will create a fun and inviting atmosphere as kids enter your area and gather in their Fiesta Crews.

Ten minutes before your VBS is scheduled to start, take requests for favorite songs, and then sing the songs as the rest of the kids enter.

**SAY:** **It's so wonderful to see you here for another exciting day at Fiesta—where kids are fired up about Jesus!** Ask kids to shout, "We're fired up about Jesus!" as they crouch low and then jump up high. **Let's sing "Never Be the Same!" so everyone knows our Fiesta is beginning!**

Lead "Never Be the Same!" The words and motions are on page 52.

## FIESTA FINDINGS

*By the middle of the week, we could have hosted an all-requests hour of Sing & Play Olé! Kids came up to the leader throughout the VBS and asked her to "please, please, please" let them sing certain songs. If possible, allow time in your schedule for kids to sing their favorite songs. (After all, how can you tell kids no when they really want to worship?)*

# DAY 4

## FIESTA FINDINGS

*One parent was amazed that her young, shy child wanted to pray out loud at a restaurant. What a way to show that Jesus is our leader!*

## RED HOT TIPS

*The Daily Challenge is a way for kids to put the Bible Point into practice every day. Remember to keep the focus on the joy we get from serving and loving others. Although it might be easy to slip and point out our "good deeds," be sure, instead, to show kids how easy and fun it is to share God's love and put their faith in action.*

**SAY:** Great singing! Yesterday we learned that 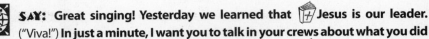 Jesus is our leader. ("Viva!") **In just a minute, I want you to talk in your crews about what you did for your Daily Challenges. How did you show others that** Jesus is our leader? ("Viva!") Give a personal example. You might tell kids that you said a prayer that everyone at VBS would know that Jesus is their leader. ("Viva!")

Hold up a Daily Challenge Flag. **SAY: Take out the Daily Challenge Flag from your Crew Bag. Then, crew members, take turns telling your crew how you showed others that** Jesus is our leader. ("Viva!")

After a minute, take the microphone around to the children, and let several children tell about ways they showed others that Jesus is their leader.

**SAY: Great ways to show others that** Jesus is our leader! ("Viva!") **Now, we're going to lower the lines of our Daily Challenge Poles. The Materials Manager from your crew will tape the flag to the line. We'll sing a song and raise the flags high to show others that we know** Jesus is our leader! ("Viva!") **By tomorrow we'll see so many of these flags flying! We're so fired up about Jesus, we want everyone to be fired up about him, too.**

**Let's sing "We Want to See Jesus Lifted High."**

**CD Track 4** Sing "We Want to See Jesus Lifted High," and watch the flags go up!

**SAY: Today we're going to learn that** Jesus is our Savior! ("Viva!") **How about you *kids* shouting the Bible Point so all of us leaders and adults shout "Viva!" Ready?** Wait for kids to shout, "Jesus is our Savior!" Then you and the adults respond with "Viva!"

**We need a Bible Memory Buddy to help us remember that** Jesus is our Savior. ("Viva!") **But first, let's get the other Bible Memory Buddies front and center!**

Ask a volunteer to hold the picture of Ray, and have kids say that day's Bible Point: Jesus is our friend. ("Viva!") Ask another volunteer to hold the blanket close by Ray, and let the kids tell you about the men who took their friend to Jesus for healing.

**Who remembers the next day's Bible Memory Buddy?** Ask a volunteer to hold up a poster of Rosa, and have kids say that day's Bible Point: Jesus is our life. ("Viva!") Ask a child to wrap up in the sheet, and let the kids tell you about Jesus raising Lazarus from the dead.

**Who remembers yesterday's Bible Memory Buddy?** Ask a volunteer to hold up a poster of Cody, and have kids say yesterday's Bible Point: Jesus is our leader. ("Viva!") Give a volunteer the fishing net, and let kids tell you about the disciples dropping their nets and following Jesus.

**Today's Bible Point is** Jesus is our Savior. ("Viva!") **What Bible Memory Buddy can help us remember our Bible Point? I know! Spike!** Ask a volunteer to hold up Spike's poster. **Look at Spike. He's a cactus.**

**Look at how Spike's arms are bit like a cross shape. He also has sharp needles. Spike reminds us of the sharp nails that put Jesus on a cross. Spike reminds us that** Jesus is our Savior. ("Viva!") **Today we'll learn about Jesus dying and then rising again.** Ask a volunteer to hold a cross. **Jesus died on a cross and then rose to heaven! We need Jesus to take away our sins so we can be with God in heaven.**

**Let's sing a song called "You Gave" as a prayer to thank Jesus for giving his life and saving us.**

Think sharp! Tell everyone Jesus is our Savior!

**Track 9** Lead the kids in singing "You Gave." Show how to motion "yesterday" by placing a fist close to your cheek and moving it backward. The words and motions are on page 62.

*The first time the kids sang "You Gave," they sounded like they'd been singing it since the beginning of the week. They caught on so quickly, and they sang so sweetly. It sounded like we had a room full of angels!*

**"Yesterday" (step 1)**

**"Yesterday" (step 2)**

**SAY:** Wow! Jesus gave his life for us, and he lives forever. Jesus did that for each of us so we could be with God forever.

Bring out your Bible, and **SAY: The Bible says that** Jesus is our Savior! ("Viva!") **Today's Treasure Verse from the Bible is found in John 4:19. The Treasure Verse says, "Since I live, you also will live."** Ask kids to follow your motions. Raise both hands high for "Since I live," point to everyone on "you," and raise your arms high again for "also will live."

**"Since I live,**

**you**

**also will live."**

**Wow! Because Jesus lives, we will, too—forever! It's time for the Fiesta Crew Leaders to go out for a huddle and a prayer. We love you! The rest of us will sing "Help Me, Jesus." We never have to be afraid of death or anything because of Jesus. Jesus helps us live each day on earth, and we'll be with him and everyone who believes in him one day in heaven.**

**Track 10** Lead the kids in singing "Help Me, Jesus" (Hebrews 13:6). The words and motions are on page 63.

When you finish singing, **SAY: Remember that** Jesus is our Savior! ("Viva!") **He helps us throughout our days on earth until we get to live with him forever!**

Introduce the director who will make announcements, ask a Prayer Person to pray, and dismiss the kids to their stations. Play the *Sing & Play Olé Music* CD as the children leave the Sing & Play Olé area.

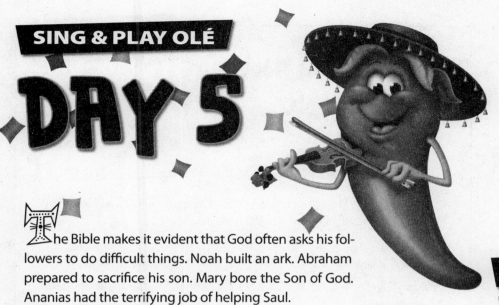

## SING & PLAY OLÉ

# DAY 5

The Bible makes it evident that God often asks his followers to do difficult things. Noah built an ark. Abraham prepared to sacrifice his son. Mary bore the Son of God. Ananias had the terrifying job of helping Saul.

To understand Ananias' fear, it's important to realize just how much Saul hated Christians. He approved the stoning of Stephen, arrested Christians in Jerusalem, and was in the process of expanding his reach to Damascus. Saul was the man you ran *away* from—not *to*! So it's understandable that when God called Ananias to restore Saul's sight, Ananias was hesitant. Despite his fear, Ananias embraced Saul, calling him brother and placing his hands on Saul. Assisted by Ananias' faith and servanthood, Saul changed forever.

God is asking the kids in your church to do difficult things, too. Maybe God is prodding someone to reach out to a lonely classmate. Perhaps God is nudging a child to obey his or her parents. Or it might be that God is asking a child to stop saying bad words. Whatever the task, kids need to know that Jesus is there to help them every step of the way. Use the activities in today's lesson to give kids confidence that Jesus will help them do anything God asks!

☀ Because [+] Jesus is our helper, we can

- face difficulties with confidence,

- follow God fearlessly, and

- rely on him to get us through hard times.

## BIBLE POINT:

[+] Jesus is our helper.

## TREASURE VERSE:

"The Lord is my helper, so I will have no fear" *(Hebrews 13:6).*

## BIBLE STORY:

Ananias helps Saul *(Acts 9:1-19).*

## DAY 5 BIBLE POINT

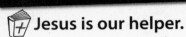 Jesus is our helper.

# Frieda's Fiesta Adventure (Day 5)

**Bible Point:**  Jesus is our helper.

> **Props**
> *Frieda is dressed in full tourist gear, with sunglasses and sun hat, and carrying her bags of souvenirs. In one of the bags is a pair of ski boots.*

*(Frieda and Leader enter from opposite sides and meet center stage.)*

**Frieda:** *(Hugs Leader.)* This has been the *best* week of my life in this wonderful Fiesta village.

**Leader:** I'm glad.

**Frieda:** You and all my friends here at Fiesta taught me that Jesus is my friend. *(Pauses while kids say "Viva!")* You welcomed me when I felt alone.

**Leader:** I learned something, too. I learned that God brings me good friends. You are *mi amiga*, Frieda.

**Frieda:** And you are *mi amiga*. You gave me a place to live and told me about Jesus. I also learned that Jesus is my life. *(Pause while kids say "Viva!")* Jesus is more important to me than shopping. Which reminds me…I want to give you something. I brought it along from Wisconsin just in case.

*(Frieda pulls ski boots from one of her bags and then hands the ski boots to the Leader.)*

**Leader:** Thank you…but what are these?

**Frieda:** Ski boots. You can't be too prepared when you travel, you know. When you're stuck in the snow, nothing helps like a good pair of boots.

**Leader:** You're very kind, but in our Fiesta village it rarely, if ever, snows.

**Frieda:** Then bring them with you when *you* come to visit *me*. You're always welcome in Wackanack, Wisconsin. Come in the winter, and I'll help you learn to ski. *(Sound effect of bus starting up with a rumble.)* Oh! I have to hurry and thank you more before the bus leaves without me again! *(To kids)* Thank you for teaching me that Jesus is our leader. *(Pauses while kids say "Viva!")* Jesus always points us in the right direction.

**Leader:** I'm going to start pointing you in the direction of your bus. *(Sound effect of bus rumbling again.)* Next time you visit us, bring your husband and show him all the sites.

**Frieda:** *(Leaning back into the Leader as the Leader pushes her toward stage right and the waiting bus.)* I also wanted to thank you for telling me that Jesus is our Savior. *(Pauses while kids say "Viva!")* What would we do without Jesus who loves us so much?

**Leader:** We need Jesus to save us. And we also need to know that Jesus is our helper. ("Viva!") Jesus will help you tell others about him, and he will help you live each day of your life.

**Frieda:** I thank God that Jesus is my helper. ("Viva!") And I thank God that you've been such a wonderful helper to me, too. You all helped take care of me this week. You helped me learn new things. You helped me make friends with Jesus.

*(Sound effect of bus rumble changes as the bus starts pulling away.)*

**Leader:** And I helped you know the bus is leaving without you.

**Frieda:** Right. You'd help me know if a bus was going to leave without me someday.

**Leader:** No, I mean right *now*. The bus is leaving without you!

**Frieda:** *(Looking stage right.)* What? It's leaving! *(Giving the Leader a quick hug, waving to the kids, and then grabbing bags and dashing off stage right.)* I'll see you in Wackanack!

**Leader:** Goodbye, friend!

**Frieda:** *(From off stage.)* Come see me this Christmas! We'll play in the snow!

*(Bus fades into distance.)*

**Leader:** Isn't God good? He gave us friends this whole week, and he gave us Jesus. We're so fired up about our friend Jesus! Let's sing some songs about Jesus right now!

# Firing Up for Fiesta

Before the kids arrive, check to make sure that all of the equipment is set up and working. About 15 minutes before your VBS is scheduled to start, begin playing the *Sing & Play Olé Music* CD. The songs will create a fun and inviting atmosphere as kids enter your area and gather in their Fiesta Crews.

Ten minutes before your VBS is scheduled to start, take requests for favorite songs, and sing the songs as the rest of the kids enter.

**SAY: Welcome once again to Sing & Play Olé at Fiesta—where kids are fired up about Jesus!** Ask kids to shout, "We're fired up about Jesus!" as they crouch low and then jump up high. **Let's sing "Never Be the Same!" so everyone knows Fiesta is beginning!**

Lead "Never Be the Same!" The words and motions are on page 52.

**SAY: I'm so fired up about Jesus! Because of him, we'll never be the same! Yesterday we learned that Jesus is our Savior.** ("Viva!") **In just a minute, I want you to talk in your crews about what you did for your Daily Challenges. How did you show others that Jesus is our Savior?** ("Viva!") Give a personal example, such as e-mailing a friend to describe the awesome week at Fiesta.

Hold up a Daily Challenge Flag.

**SAY: Take the Daily Challenge Flag from your Crew Bag. Then take turns telling your crew how you showed others that Jesus is our Savior.** ("Viva!")

### RED HOT TIPS

*If some crews haven't had a chance to sit near the front, be sure to move crews around today.*

### RED HOT TIPS

*As the kids arrive, have the Fiesta Crew Leaders remind them of their jobs. If the crews receive new children, or if the kids want to trade jobs, Fiesta Crew Leaders can reassign the jobs and remind the children of their duties.*

After a minute, take the microphone around to the children, and let several children tell about ways they showed others that Jesus is their Savior.

**SAY:** **Great ways to show others that** Jesus is our Savior! ("Viva!") **Now, we're going to lower the lines of our Daily Challenge Poles. The Materials Manager from your crew will tape the flag to the line. We'll sing a song and raise the flags high to show others that we know** Jesus is our Savior. ("Viva!"). **We'll see so many of these banners flying! We're so fired up about Jesus that we want everyone else to be fired up about him, too.**

**Let's sing "We Want to See Jesus Lifted High."**

Sing "We Want to See Jesus Lifted High," and watch the flags go up!

**Today we're going to learn that** Jesus is our helper! ("Viva!")

**We need a Bible Memory Buddy to help us remember today's Bible Point. But first, let's get the other Bible Memory Buddies front and center!**

Ask a volunteer to hold the picture of Ray, and have kids say that day's Bible Point: Jesus is our friend. ("Viva!") Ask another volunteer to hold the blanket close by Ray. **We learned about the men who took their friend on a mat to Jesus for healing.**

**Who remembers the next day's Bible Memory Buddy?** Ask a volunteer to hold up a poster of Rosa, and have kids say that day's Bible Point: Jesus is our life. ("Viva!") Ask a child to wrap up in the sheet. **We learned about Jesus raising Lazarus from the dead.**

**Who remembers the next day's Bible Memory Buddy?** Ask a volunteer to hold up a poster of Cody, and have kids say that day's Bible Point: Jesus is our leader. ("Viva!") Give a volunteer the fishing net. **We learned that when Jesus called his disciples, they dropped their fishing nets and followed their leader!**

**Who remembers yesterday's Bible Point?** Ask a volunteer to hold up a poster of Spike, and have kids say that day's Bible Point: Jesus is our Savior. ("Viva!") Give a volunteer a cross to hold. **We learned that Jesus died and rose again. Because of Jesus, we will live forever.**

**What Bible Memory Buddy can help us remember that** Jesus is our helper! ("Viva!") **I know! Pablo, the chili pepper!** Ask a volunteer to hold up Pablo's poster.

**Chili peppers help add spice and flavor to food. Pablo reminds us that** Jesus is our helper! ("Viva!") **Today we'll learn about Saul, a mean man who hurt Jesus' followers. One day, Saul was blinded by a bright light.** Ask a volunteer to stand in front and wear large sunglasses. Ask another volunteer to stand close by. **The bright light was Jesus, who wanted to know why Saul was hurting people and hurting Jesus. Jesus helped a man named Ananias help Saul see again.** Ask the other volunteer to take off "Saul's" sunglasses.

**Let's sing "Help Me, Jesus" and thank Jesus for helping us be brave and not afraid.**

Lead kids in singing "Help Me, Jesus" (Hebrews 13:6). Words and motions are on page 63.

Knowing that Jesus is my helper adds spice to my life!

**SAY:** Today's Treasure Verse from the Bible comes from Hebrews 13:6. The Treasure Verse says, **"The Lord is my helper, so I will have no fear."** Have kids follow your motions. Raise both hands high for "The Lord is my helper," and then make muscleman arms, one arm and then the other, on "have no fear."

**"The Lord is my helper,        so I will have no fear."**

**Now it's time for our helpful Fiesta Crew Leaders to go out for a huddle and a prayer! Thanks for helping us know more about Jesus!**

Host an all-requests singing time while the leaders huddle.

When the leaders return from huddling and praying, invite the director to give announcements, close in prayer, and then dismiss the children. Play the *Sing & Play Olé Music* CD as the kids leave the Sing & Play Olé area.

# Sing & Play Olé
# Song Lyrics & Motions

# Never Be the Same!

(Chorus)

| | |
|---|---|
| Come on, let's have some fun. | *(Motion "come here," one hand at a time.)* |
| It's all about Jesus' love! | *(Motion "Jesus" by pointing one middle finger to the palm of the other hand and then pointing the other middle finger to the other palm; motion "love" by crossing your arms on your chest.)* |
| We're here to praise his name. | *(Make fists and circle them up high.)* |
| We'll never be the same! | *(Shake your head "no.")* |

(Verse)

| | |
|---|---|
| Jesus is our friend. | *(Shake a neighbor's hand.)* |
| He is our helper. | |
| We will follow him; | *(March in place.)* |
| He is the King of kings! | *(Form a K by placing your thumb between your pointer and middle fingers, and move your hand from your shoulder to your hip.)* |
| He is our life. | *(Form Ls with both pointer fingers and thumbs, hands at hip level, and lift both hands up.)* |
| He is our Savior. | *(Make fists and stretch your arms to the side to form a cross.)* |
| We are here to praise his name! | *(Make fists and circle them high.)* |

(Sing chorus.)

| | |
|---|---|
| Cha ch-ch-cha cha cha cha cha ch-ch-cha fiesta! | *(Face one direction and put your hands on the shoulders of the person in front of you. Raise both hands high on "Fiesta!")* |
| Cha ch-ch-cha cha cha cha cha ch-ch-cha fiesta! | |
| Cha ch-ch-cha cha cha cha cha ch-ch-cha fiesta! | *(Go the other direction with the same motions.)* |
| Cha ch-ch-cha cha cha cha cha ch-ch-cha fiesta! | |

# No, Not One/What a Friend We Have in Jesus

No, not one; no, not one;

No, not…no, not…no, not…no, not one.

There's not a friend like the lowly Jesus.

*(Shake your "no," and raise one finger high on "one.")*

*(For "friend," hook pointer fingers together. Motion "Jesus" by pointing one middle finger to the other palm and then pointing the other middle finger to the palm of the first hand.)*

No, not one; no, not one.

No one else can heal all our souls' diseases.

No, not one; no, not one.

*(Pat a back.)*

Oh, Jesus knows all about our struggles;

*(Motion "Jesus," and then motion "struggles" by pointing pointer fingers horizontally and moving them back and forth.)*

He will guide until the day is done.

*(Motion "day" by forming a D with your pointer finger up and the other fingers in a circle, and bring the D downward.)*

There's not a friend like the lowly Jesus.

No, not one; no, not one;

Oh, no, not one; no, not one.

No, not one; no, not one;

No, not…no, not…no, not…no, not one.

What a friend we have in Jesus,

*(For "friend," hook both pointer fingers together, and then motion "Jesus.")*

All our sins and griefs to bear!

*(Make fists and stretch them to the sides to form a cross.)*

What a privilege to carry

*(Rock your arms back and forth as if carrying something.)*

Everything to God in prayer.

*(Put your hands together as if praying, and raise them high.)*

Oh, Jesus knows all about our struggles.

He will guide until the day is done.

There's not a friend like the lowly Jesus.

No, not one; no, not one;

No, not one; no, not one;

No, not one; no, not one.

# I Have a Friend (Yo Tengo un Amigo)

I have a friend who loves me,

*(Raise your fist high on "I"; hook your pointer fingers together on "friend"; cross your arms over your chest on "loves"; and place both hands on your chest for "me.")*

Who loves me, who loves me.

*(Cross your arms over your chest on "loves"; place both hands on your chest for "me.")*

I have a friend who loves me,

*(Raise your fist high on "I"; hook your pointer fingers together on "friend"; cross your arms over your chest on "loves"; and place both hands on your chest for "me.")*

And Jesus is his name.

*(Motion "Jesus" by pointing one middle finger to the palm of the other hand and then pointing the other middle finger to the other palm; then make Xs with your pointer and middle fingers, and raise them high for "is his name.")*

*(Repeat.)*

He loves me; he loves me;

*(Cross your arms over your chest on "loves," and place both hands on your chest for "me.")*

He loves me with such tender love.

*(Hug yourself on "with such tender love.")*

He loves me; he loves me,

*(Cross your arms over your chest on "loves," and place both hands on chest for "me.")*

And Jesus is his name.

*(Motion "Jesus" by pointing one middle finger to the palm of the other hand and then pointing the other middle finger to the other palm; make Xs with your pointer middle fingers, and raise them high for "is his name.")*

and

Yo tengo un amigo que me ama;

*(Repeat the above motions with the Spanish version.)*

me ama; me ama.

Yo tengo un amigo que me ama;

Su nombre es Jesus.

Que me ama; me ama; me ama;

Con tierno amor.

Me ama; me ama;

Su nombre es Jesus.

*(Repeat English verses.)*

# We Want to See Jesus Lifted High

We want to see…we want to see…　　　　　*(Place both hands over your eyes on "see.")*
We want to see Jesus lifted high!　　　　　*(Raise your hands high on "Jesus lifted high.")*
We want to see…we want to see…
We want to see Jesus lifted…
Jesus lifted…Jesus lifted high!

We want to see Jesus lifted high,
A banner that flies across the land,　　　　*(Move your hands in an arc from left to right.)*
That people will see the truth and know　　　*(Point to your eyes for "see," and point to your head for "know.")*
He is the way to heaven.　　　　　　　　　*(Move your hands in an arc from right to left.)*
*(Repeat.)*

We want to see *(clap, clap, clap)*,
We want to see *(clap, clap, clap)*,
We want to see Jesus lifted high!
*(Repeat.)*

We want to see Jesus lifted high,
A banner that flies across the land,
That people will see the truth and know
He is the way to heaven.

We want to see *(we want to see)*,
We want to see *(we want to see)*,
We want to see Jesus lifted high!
*(Repeat twice.)*

We want to see *(we want to see)*,
We want to see *(we want to see)*,
We want to see Jesus lifted,
Jesus lifted,
Jesus lifted high!

# I've Got the Joy

I like to sing (sing),                         (Cup both hands by your mouth, and then move both hands out.)

'Cause I got the joy.                          (Pat both hands on your chest.)

I like to sing (sing),

'Cause I got the joy.

I like to sing, sing, sing,

'Cause I got the joy;

I got the joy of the Lord in my heart.         (Use both hands to shape a heart.)


I like to clap (clap) my hands,                (Clap your hands, and then hold them out.)

'Cause I got the joy.                           (Pat both hands on your chest.)

I like to clap (clap) my hands,

'Cause I got the joy.

I like to clap my hands (clap),

'Cause I got the joy.

I've got the joy of the Lord in my heart.      (Use both hands to shape a heart.)


(Chorus)

I'm gonna share the joy everywhere that I go,   (March in place while you move both arms out.)

And I'm gonna share the joy with everybody I know.   (Keep marching in place while you point to people.)

I'm gonna share the joy every night and day.    (Crouch low on "night" and stretch high on "day.")

I can't keep it to myself; I got to give it away!    (Hug yourself on "keep" and extend both arms on "give.")


I like to jump (jump, jump!),                   (Jump in place.)

'Cause I got the joy.

I like to jump (jump, jump!),

'Cause I got the joy.

I like to jump, jump, jump,

'Cause I got the joy.

I've got the joy of the Lord in my heart.

I like to shout *(shout!)*                    *(Punch a fist high.)*

'Cause I got the joy.

I like to shout *(shout!)*

'Cause I got the joy.

I like to shout, shout, shout!

'Cause I got the joy.

I've got the joy of the Lord in my heart.


*(Sing chorus.)*


I like to sing *(sing)*

I like to clap *(clap)*

I like to jump *(jump, jump!)*,

I like to shout *(shout!)*

*(Repeat.)*

# King Jesus Is All

Yeah, yeah, yeah,

Yeah, yeah, yeah,

Yeah, yeah, yeah, yeah, yeah, yeah,

Yeah, yeah, yeah,

Yeah, yeah, yeah, yeah, yeah, yeah.

*(Nod your head while you dance freestyle.)*

King Jesus is all *(King Jesus is all)*,

*(Motion "all" by scooping with one hand, and placing the back of that hand in the palm of the other.)*

My all in all *(my all in all)*.

*(Motion "all.")*

And I know that he'll answer *(and I know that he'll answer)*

*(Point to your head on "know," and then place both pointer fingers to lips and move them out for "answer.")*

Me when I call *(me when I call)*.

*(Make praying hands.)*

Walking by my side *(walking by my side)*,

*(March in place.)*

I'm satisfied *(I'm satisfied)*.

*(Make an "OK" sign.)*

King Jesus is all *(King Jesus is all)*,

*(Motion "all.")*

My all in all *(my all in all)*.

*(Motion "all.")*

*(Repeat.)*

# Trading My Sorrows

I'm trading my sorrows;          *(Push both hands, palms out, to one side as if pushing something away.)*

I'm trading my shame;          *(Push the opposite direction.)*

I'm laying them down          *(Motion both hands, palms up, as if laying something down.)*

For the joy of the Lord.          *(Wave both hands side to side overhead.)*


I'm trading my sickness;          *(Repeat above motions.)*

I'm trading my pain;

I'm laying them down

For the joy of the Lord.


Yes, Lord; yes, Lord;          *(Give a thumbs-up sign for "yes," and form an L with both pointer fingers and thumbs for "Lord.")*

Yes, yes, Lord.

Yes, Lord; yes, Lord;

Yes, yes, Lord.

Yes, Lord; yes, Lord;

Yes, yes, Lord.

Amen.          *(Put your hands together as if praying.)*


*(Repeat from the beginning.)*


Yes, Lord; yes Lord;

Yes, yes, Lord.

Yes, Lord; yes, Lord;

Yes, yes, Lord.

Yes, Lord; yes, Lord;

Yes, yes, Lord.

Amen.

*(Repeat.)*

# I'm Gonna Clap My Hands

| | |
|---|---|
| I'm gonna clap my hands | *(Clap your hands.)* |
| To show I love you. | *(Reach both hands out to the side, and then raise them high.)* |
| Gonna shout out loud; | *(Punch your fists in the air.)* |
| Gonna sing your praise. | *(Make fists and circle them high.)* |
| You are everything to me. | *(Raise you hands high, and then bring them to your chest.)* |
| Jesus, I love your name; | *(Motion "Jesus" by pointing one middle finger to the palm of the other hand and then pointing the other middle finger to the other palm, and cross your arms over your chest and jump in a circle.)* |
| I love your name. | *(Keep jumping.)* |
| | |
| I'm gonna stamp my feet | *(Stamp your feet.)* |
| To show I love you. | *(Reach both hands out to the side, and then raise them high.)* |
| Gonna jump around; | *(Jump.)* |
| Gonna sing your praise. | *(Make fists, and circle them high.)* |
| You are everything to me | *(Raise both hands high, and then bring them to your chest.)* |
| Jesus, I love your name; | *(Motion "Jesus" by pointing one middle finger to the palm of the other hand and then pointing the other middle finger to the other palm; cross your arms over your chest and jump in a circle.)* |
| I love your name. | *(Keep jumping.)* |
| | |
| You are the best friend | *(Hook your pointer fingers together.)* |
| That I could ever know. | *(Point to your head.)* |
| I lift my hands to you | *(Lift your hands.)* |
| 'Cause you died for me upon the cross. | *(Place both fists on your chest for "me," and then extend them out to your sides for "cross.")* |
| You took away my sin and shame. | *(Make a throwing away motion.)* |
| | |
| I'm gonna clap my hands | |
| To show I love you. | |
| Gonna shout out loud; | |

Gonna sing your praise.

You are everything to me.

Jesus, I love you.

I'm gonna stamp my feet

To show I love you.

Gonna jump around;

Gonna sing your praise.

You are everything to me.

Jesus, I love your name.

I love your name.

I love your name.

I love your name.

# You Gave

Lord, I want to be
*(Form an L with your pointer finger and thumb, and raise it high. Then bring both arms in to yourself for "want.")*

Pleasing to you
*(Use one hand to "draw" a circle on your chest.)*

In everything I do.
*(Reach both hands out.)*

And I want to love you more,
*(Cross your arms over your chest.)*

More than yesterday,
*(Place one fist by your cheek, and then move it back.)*

More than words can say,
*(Place both pointer fingers by your lips, and then move them out.)*


'Cause you gave your life;
*(Motion both hands out as if giving something.)*

You lived and died for me, for me.
*(Reach both fists out to form a cross, and then place your hands on your chest.)*

You paid the price;
*(Place your right middle finger on the left palm. With a deliberate movement, brush the right palm against the left—as if wiping it clean.)*

You sacrificed for me, for me.
*(Place both hands on your chest.)*

And now the least that I can do
*(Hold both hands out to the sides.)*

Is live my life for you.
*(Place both hands on your chest as you bow your head.)*


*(Repeat from the beginning.)*

# Help Me, Jesus (Hebrews 13:6)

Oh, yeah!

*(Crouch low, and then raise your arms high.)*

When you help me, Jesus, oh-oh-oh-oh,

*(Place a fist on the other palm, and lift both hands up. Move your shoulders and hands up and down to the beat.)*

I am not afraid.

*(Shake your head "no.")*

When you help me, Jesus, oh-oh-oh-oh,

*(Place a fist on the other palm, and lift both hands up. Move your shoulders and hands up and down to the beat.)*

I am always brave.

*(Make muscleman arms.)*

When you help me, Jesus, oh-oh-oh-oh,

I am not afraid.

When you help me, help me, Jesus,

I am always brave, and I am not afraid.


*(Repeat from the beginning.)*

# Sing & Play Olé

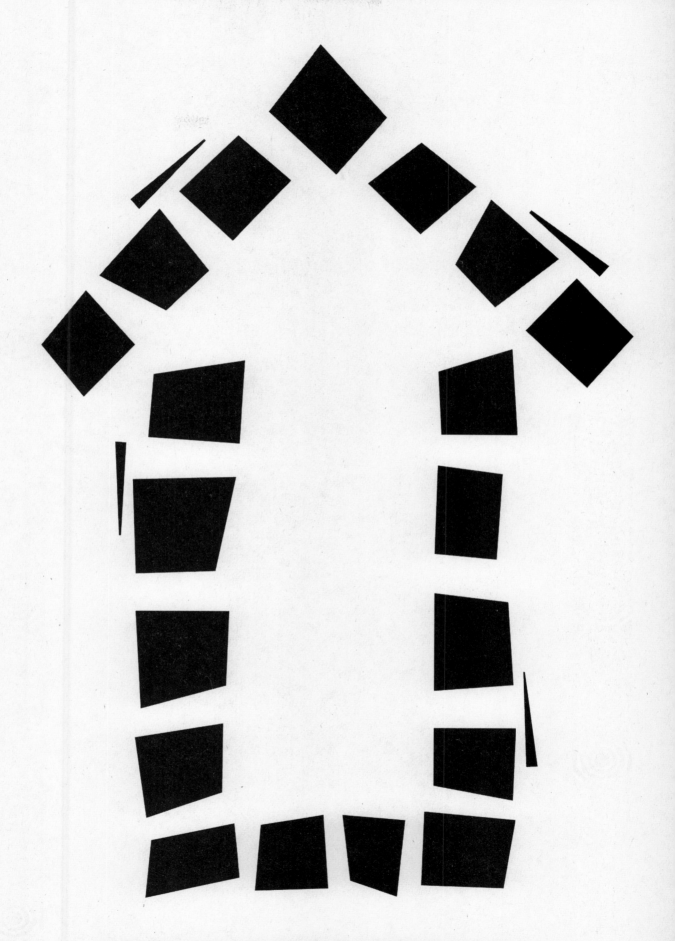

Group's

# Fiesta!™

### Where kids are fired up about Jesus

# Sing & Play Olé

## MUSIC

# Never Be the Same!

# Never Be the Same!

# Never Be the Same!

Cha ch-ch-cha cha cha cha ch-cha    cha ch-ch-cha fi-es-ta!

Cha ch-ch-cha cha cha cha ch-cha    cha ch-ch-cha fi-es-ta!    Cha ch-ch-cha cha cha cha ch-cha

cha ch-ch-cha fi-es-ta!    Cha ch-ch-cha cha cha cha ch-cha    cha ch-ch-cha fi-es-ta!

# Never Be the Same!

# Never Be the Same!

# No, Not One/What a Friend We Have in Jesus

# No, Not One/What a Friend We Have in Jesus

# No, Not One/What a Friend We Have in Jesus

# No, Not One/What a Friend We Have in Jesus

# I Have a Friend (Yo Tengo un Amigo)

# I Have a Friend (Yo Tengo un Amigo)

# I Have a Friend (Yo Tengo un Amigo)

# We Want to See Jesus Lifted High

# We Want to See Jesus Lifted High

# We Want to See Jesus Lifted High

# I've Got the Joy

# I've Got the Joy

I got the joy.__ I like to clap (clap) my hands, 'cause I got the joy.__ I like to clap my hands 'cause

I got the joy.__ I've got the joy of the Lord__ in my heart__ I'm

gon-na share the joy ev-'ry-where that I go, and I'm gon - - na share the joy with ev-'ry - bod-y I know. I'm

gon-na share the joy ev-'ry night and day. I can't keep it to my-self; I got to give it a - way!__

# I've Got the Joy

# I've Got the Joy

I like to sing (sing).___ I like to clap (clap).

I like to jump (jump, jump!). I like to

shout (shout!). I like to

# King Jesus Is All

# King Jesus Is All

# Trading My Sorrows

I'm trad-ing my___ sor - rows;  I'm trad-ing my___ shame;___
I'm trad ing my___ sick - ness;  I'm trad ing my___ pain;___

I'm lay-ing them down   for the joy of the   Lord.
I'm lay-ing them down   for the joy of the

# Trading My Sorrows

# Trading My Sorrows

# Trading My Sorrows

# I'm Gonna Clap My Hands

# I'm Gonna Clap My Hands

# I'm Gonna Clap My Hands

# I'm Gonna Clap My Hands

# You Gave

Lord, I want to be___ pleas ing to you in ev - 'ry thing I do.

And I want to love you more,___ more than yes - ter - day,___ more than words can say, 'cause you

gave your life; you lived and died for me,___ for me.___ You

# You Gave

# You Gave

# You Gave

me._____ And now the least that I can do is live my___ life for

you.

# Help Me, Jesus (Hebrews 13:6)

# Help Me, Jesus (Hebrews 13:6)

# Help Me, Jesus (Hebrews 13:6)